# CHARLTON HESTON

*Also by Michael Munn*

**KIRK DOUGLAS**

# CHARLTON
# HESTON

## MICHAEL MUNN

**St. Martin's Press**
**New York**

Library of Congress Cataloging in Publication Data

Munn, Michael.
    Charlton Heston.

    1. Heston, Charlton.    2.  Moving-picture actors and
actresses—United States—Biography.    I. Title.
PN2287.H47M86    1986        791.43′028′0924    [B]    86-13124
ISBN 0-312-13067-8

First published in Great Britain by Robson Books Ltd.

First U.S. Edition

10 9 8 7 6 5 4 3 2 1

This book is for my dear parents.

# Contents

# Introduction

IT WAS LATE IN 1976 WHEN I FIRST MET CHARLTON HESTON. HE was in London promoting *Midway*, and he wore the beard he'd grown for *Gray Lady Down*. He was in London just long enough to see journalists interested in him. I imagine that included every single Fleet Street reporter, every radio and TV interviewer and every magazine journalist.

His tight schedule allowed him to see only a selected number of all those, and I was lucky to be included as a staff writer for *Film Review* magazine.

Now I have to be frank and admit that this was something I'd long waited for. Since I saw *Ben-Hur* as a child, Heston had been my idol. So this, as far as I was concerned, was the most important assignment I'd yet been given. I had a million questions to ask, and just half an hour to ask them all in. But what I hadn't counted on was being the last in a long line of interviewers. And the lady journalist in front of me went way over schedule, gradually whittling down my allotted time. I eventually ended up with just twenty minutes. And I had all those questions!

I was surprised to find that Heston's suite at the Dorchester Hotel was not the kind of luxurious, exotic millionaire's suite complete with sunken bath and hanging chandelier that one tends to expect from rich Hollywood movie stars. It was comparatively modest, and the large frame of Heston seemed to fill the small lounge.

I admit I was excited. I confess I was nervous. But what really dampened the ensuing interview was that he was just plain tired; tired of talking to strangers all day, of answering a thousand questions (many of them the same old questions). It must be said that being the renowned professional that he is, Charlton Heston is always totally gracious to those in his presence and does his best to accommodate the press. I recall about six months earlier I had called him on the telephone when he was in England making *The Prince and The Pauper*. I was put straight through to his room and was surprised to

7

find myself talking to the man himself rather than to some press agent or secretary strategically placed by the phone to intercept all incoming calls. I'd explained who I was and asked for an interview, and in his usual courteous manner, he had said, 'I am really sorry, but we've finished on the film here and I'm flying home first thing in the morning. Otherwise I'd have been glad to see you. Next time I'm in town on business, we'll try and arrange something.'

Now he was in town, and quite exhausted. And all I had was twenty minutes to get a full-feature interview. From the first, things did not bode well. He talked a little about *Midway* with no obvious personal enthusiasm for the picture.

Then I brought up his own labour of love of some years previous, *Antony and Cleopatra* which had been both a critical and commercial flop. However, I admired the film greatly, and told him so. Now he began to warm up, and I decided to play my ace. Every interviewer should keep an ace up his sleeve.

I said, 'Of course, *Antony And Cleopatra* wasn't the first time you'd been behind the cameras, was it?'

He looked puzzled. 'I've directed on the stage before,' he said. 'What had you in mind?'

'*The Greatest Story Ever Told*,' I replied. Even just to mention that film to any of the hundreds of actors who appeared in it was risky, since very few of its huge cast ever had anything good to say about it. So I had no idea if I'd touched a raw nerve, and I also prayed that I'd done my homework correctly.

He suddenly threw back his head, laughed loudly and slapped his knee.

'By God!' he boomed. 'You *are* sharp. You're absolutely right. I'd forgotten that I directed one scene in that film – the one where the Baptist [Heston played this role] is arrested.'

He then proceeded to give me a wonderful anecdote, and things looked good.

But the time was almost spent. I mentioned the name of Tom Gries, who'd directed three of Heston's pictures – although only the first, *Will Penny*, was memorable.

His response was, 'Did you know that Tom died three days ago?'

That was about the end of the interview, and I came away with little that was quotable. I did manage to get a feature out of it, though only just.

But it was a disappointment. Heston has always been one of those personalities considered interview-proof; that is to say, you shouldn't be able to fail to get a good interview from him. And yet this had not been good. I had seen him interviewed on television many times, and had even been at a recording of an hour-long interview he did with Michael Parkinson several years earlier, and he had always been articulate, precise, concise and quotable.

I had also noticed, particularly at the Parkinson recording, that he formed a relationship with the audience that was warm and immediate.

It had been a different man I had met this day.

Of course, I realize that any person who does I don't know how many interviews in one day is going to be wound down by the end of it. But what I have since discovered through personal experience is that Heston doesn't just give an interview – he *performs*. Sometimes flawlessly, sometimes poorly.

For him, doing any interview is part of the job of acting. He does it dutifully. If it is about a film he is currently working on and you are fortunate enough to see him at the studio during production, as I later did, he's full of the excitement and enthusiasm he has for the role, and it translates to the interview. And because the vast majority of his roles are of an authoritative nature, that authority carries itself over off the film set. A one-to-one interview with him then becomes an exercise in whatever subject the film or the role happens to be about. It's as though *he* is in control of the interview and you can be sure that he'll tell you exactly what he wants you to know.

But what has struck me more than anything else is that when he has an audience – even if it's a gaggle of journalists as a press call – he performs in a totally different manner in comparison to the private interview. He literally plays to the crowd and on these occasions, as when he has a television audience, he enjoys himself immensely.

What he puts over is to all intents a *performance*, and he responds to the number of the listeners, to the environment

9

and to his enthusiasm for the subject under discussion accordingly.

And so throughout the years since I first met him it has become apparent to me that the man I've interviewed on numerous occasions is not only different to a degree on each occasion, but that he is not the same man his personal friends and his family know.

In essence, in an interview, the curtain may go up but so too do the invisible barriers; he does his best to give the single interviewer or the viewing audience what they have, as it were, paid to see: the *public* person. But never the private person with any real depth. And this is because of the very nature of the man. He is an actor, but he is also incredibly and unbelievably shy.

By his own admission, he used to hate doing interviews when he first began making movies. He had to learn how to do them, and now he can do them very well, but in a style that is probably exclusively his own.

Most actors can't help but reveal their own personalities during interviews and can quite easily cope without having any words written for them; people like Kirk Douglas, Roger Moore, Tony Curtis and Michael Caine.

But Charlton Heston has his own technique which, almost literally, is to have his own script. He knows all his answers before the questions are asked. It's as though he has a mental filing system with all the necessary answers neatly put away for immediate withdrawal at a second's notice. It's something he has perfected over the years, and he can say just about anything he wants to say, despite what the interviewer asks. He is deviously clever at it, and subsequently, if you read or hear as many interviews with Charlton Heston – or indeed do them – as I have, you begin to realize that you're hearing the same answers you've heard before, almost word for word.

As he says of interviewers, 'They can't lay a glove on me.'

But if you're really lucky, you may see the actor's mask slip occasionally. As I did during one interview, again at the Dorchester, when we were interrupted by one of the staff who had been summoned because one of Heston's garments had gone missing. The familiar characteristics of controlled patience and calming authority were gone. He fussed and

10

fumed, clearly upset and annoyed with either himself or someone else for such sloppiness. Heston likes everything just *so*. He suddenly seemed a lot more vulnerable. But when the episode was over and he came back to his chair to continue with me, he was back in his familiar persona.

On another occasion, when he was over here promoting his book of published journals, he ensured that his answers to me, concerning some of his rather abrasive remarks about temperamental ladies like Sophia Loren and Ava Gardner, were frank but inoffensive. I had really to press him to get him to be more hard-nosed about them.

Yet when our interview was momentarily interrupted by a phone call from a personal friend of his, I heard him say with a flippant chuckle, 'Poor Ava is gonna die when she reads this book.'

There was never ever any such flippancy in his remarks to me, which is to his credit. Because as a professional, if he isn't able to handle anything in a manner that meets his own stringent set of high standards, then he won't generally do it at all.

My association with Heston has always been as an interviewer so I can by no stretch of the imagination claim to *know* him. In an interview he reveals his intelligence, his opinions, his authority, even what some see as his pomposity. But he does not reveal the private man. And therein lies the challenge – what lies beneath the actor's mask that he always wears in public? And that, I hope, is what this book is all about, as well as being about his work which, as yet, I have not even acknowledged.

He has made over fifty films, won a Best Actor Oscar, appeared in a number of the most successful films of all time, is totally devoted to his profession, and remains one of the handful of Hollywood stars left whom film-makers will gamble their money on. And after a career spanning nearly forty years, that's no mean feat. He is also far more versatile than his most popular rock-jawed, haloed portrayals have displayed.

On the screen he has produced a long string of superior performances, not all of them commercially successful, such as Will Penny, General Gordon and Mark Antony, and with the exception of one London stage production in 1985, only the

11

theatre-going public of America know him to be one of the most gifted and powerful stage actors of all time. Since Laurence Olivier himself endorses that statement, I think it's safe enough.

But what motivates me more in the writing of this biography is to try and discover how a country hick from Michigan and a total misfit from Chicago could become arguably the most authoritative and influential actor to emerge from the American cinema of the late Fifties and Sixties.

And, as I have said, he is one of the most gracious of film stars, or 'public actors,' as he prefers to call himself. Some years ago when I was writing my first book, *The Great Film Epics*, he was most cooperative and helpful. But I did wonder how he would feel about someone writing his life story.

During his highly successful debut on the London stage in *The Caine Mutiny Court-Martial* in the summer of 1985, I let him know that I was writing his biography. It was, of course, with sheer delight, professionally and personally, that I received a letter from him in which he said in part, 'I want to thank you for your kind words and interest in my life... Please accept my best wishes and good luck.'

I hope that I do him justice.

MICHAEL MUNN, March 1986

# *Part One*

---

## 1

# A New Face, A New Force

THE CALIFORNIAN EVENING WAS SETTLING OVER HOLLYWOOD as the young, relatively unknown actor drove through the studios of Paramount Pictures, heading for the gate and home – if you could call an apartment in a block dominated by prostitutes 'home'! Home life was back in New York where he had a wife and a nicely burgeoning career on the stage and in live TV. Here in Hollywood he was a brand-new face on the screen with just one solitary film to his credit. And having spent the entire summer promoting that one film, he had to accept the fact that he had not set the town on fire.

Not that Paramount's publicity boys hadn't tried hard to sell him. Why, the posters for *Dark City* positively screamed, 'Take a good look at this man . . . He's a new face and a new force on the screen.'

Those may have been prophetic words, but the mediocrity of *Dark City* hardly displayed this 'new force', although the face was certainly new enough. At just twenty-six, he possessed a somewhat mature face displaying strong, almost authoritative features which belied his natural shyness. He sported a broken nose; his blue eyes were set deep beneath serious eyebrows; and a high, lined forehead was crowned with thick, light-brown, wavy hair. And only recently had his six-foot three-inch frame broadened around the chest and shoulders.

As he passed by the vast sound stages and the office complexes of Paramount Studios, he spied just ahead of him an

13

unmistakable figure. On the steps leading up to the door of his own office block stood Cecil B. De Mille, his personal secretary at his side with notebook in hand, ready to take dictation at a moment's notice or flick back through her recorded history of De Mille's more recent utterings.

De Mille's name, voice and face were as well known to the public as any of the major film stars'. He was Paramount's most powerful and prestigious producer/director, having been with the company, on and off, since its formation by Adolph Zukor in 1914. Now aged seventy, he was a sort of patriarch of Paramount, and as active in film-making as ever. He was also a most formidable figure whose very word hired and fired men on the spot.

The young actor, seeing De Mille, was faced with a sudden dilemma. Should he acknowledge the legendary director? Indeed, would De Mille know him? Or would it perhaps be best just to drive past and ignore him altogether? He had met De Mille before, at a party, but the young actor from New York was always shy at meeting people for the first time, and he was very raw and lacking in self-confidence, whereas De Mille was as old and as seasoned as the movie industry itself.

As the young actor observed, 'I was very young, and he was very old and a formidable figure.'

Almost at the last minute, the young man waved and smiled warmly at De Mille as he sped by. He just caught sight of De Mille raising his hand in return, and felt pleased he had been recognized by such a great man.

De Mille turned to his secretary. 'Who was that?' he asked.

The secretary had recognized the driver. She began flicking back through her notebook, searching for the information she knew was in there somewhere. Finding it, she said, 'His name is Charlton Heston. He's an actor from New York. Been out a few months. Made one film, *Dark City*. You ran it at the house a few weeks ago. You didn't like it.'

'Yes, I remember,' said De Mille, and added, 'but I liked the way he waved.'

Charlton Heston, totally oblivious to De Mille's observations, drove through the gates of the studio, turned into Marathon Street, and headed for his apartment, shacked up somewhere behind Grauman's Chinese Theatre.

It was not long after that that Charlton Heston flew back East to New York where his wife, Lydia, had continued playing in the same stage production she was in when her husband had been whisked off to Hollywood by Paramount producer Hal B. Wallis. Now, unsure that any kind of movie career lay ahead for him, Heston felt that there was still acting work for him in New York where over the past couple of years he had been doing very nicely. In fact, all he wanted to do was *act*, in whatever medium. He knew that movies would be a step up the ladder of security if it came off, but just to be acting and getting paid for it felt like the most wonderful thing in the world to him. That and his wife and college sweetheart, Lydia.

While Heston settled back into life on the East Coast, Cecil B. De Mille was back on the West Coast, busily engaged in preparing to make what he determined would be the biggest, most spectacular circus picture of all time, appropriately entitled *The Greatest Show on Earth*. He'd already engaged the fabulous Ringling Brothers Circus, paying them $250,000 for the use of their entire company of performers, technicians, performing animals and the big top. By the autumn of 1950 he was preoccupied with casting.

Suddenly, it was as though there was a rush for the film's roles. De Mille pictures meant mass entertainment and huge world-wide audiences. He was a master at giving the public what they wanted, and any actor eager to be in the public eye couldn't afford to turn down an offer from De Mille to be in his circus picture. Betty Hutton, for instance, went as far as sending De Mille a floral display with a tiny replica of herself swinging on a trapeze to convince him she was perfect for his film. But when De Mille met her he told her she was too big in the hips to be a trapeze artist. So she promised to slim down and that she'd fly the trapeze fearlessly if he gave her the part. He agreed.

Paulette Goddard was also anxious to be in the picture and wanted the role of the elephant girl. She sent Dr Mille an optimistic telegram reading 'HOPE ALL THOSE RUMORS ABOUT ME GOING INTO THE GREATEST SHOW ON EARTH ARE TRUE/AM RETURNING MONDAY TO SIGN CONTRACT'. However, the contract wasn't hers to sign. De Mille had given it to Gloria Grahame. Cornel Wilde was delighted when he landed the role of the Great Sebastian. His career had been ailing and needed a shot in the arm. But he was by no means De Mille's first choice for the role. Burt Lancaster was the man De Mille wanted, but Warner Brothers, who had Lancaster signed temporarily to them, wouldn't hand their star over. When it came to the role of the doctor accused of murder who hides throughout the film under heavy clown make-up, De Mille got the actor he wanted – James Stewart – and *he* wasn't desperate for work. He was enjoying the height of success at that time.

There was still the key role of Brad, the circus manager, to fill, and De Mille sought an actor for the part with the ability to be tough, demanding, authoritative and totally likeable. There was a particular young actor who seemed to stick in his memory who had waved to him one day on the Paramount lot. He began to evaluate the young man's performance in *Dark City*, and discovered that Charlton Heston had another virtually unknown film to his credit. It was a 16mm version of *Julius Caesar* with Heston portraying Mark Antony. De Mille acquired a copy of the film and ran it through. He was impressed with the amateur-made picture and with Heston's professional performance. He decided to offer Heston the part of Brad.

Heston was still in New York when his agent, Herman Citron, called with the news that De Mille wanted him for his circus picture. Heston knew immediately that this could be the big break and since he was still under contract to Hal B. Wallis and Paramount, he headed back to California, taking Lydia with him. This time Heston found a more respectable apartment where Lydia could feel comfortable while he was away shooting *The Greatest Show on Earth*, although when he went on location to places like Washington DC and Sarasota, she often went with him.

Making this film with De Mille was a vastly different experience from making *Dark City*. De Mille was a movie four-star general; a man to respect and, in some cases, to fear. He could be thoughtful and kind on the one hand, and ruthless on the other. Said Heston,

I found De Mille to be a totally gracious man, but he could

be very tough. He was hard on assistant directors and prop men and crew, but with very rare exceptions he was courteous to actors.

He would always address the extras as 'ladies and gentlemen', and he would go to some pains, if he was shooting a picture at the end of the year which required a lot of extras, to shoot scenes with the extras a week before Christmas so they had plenty of work at that time of year.

I was never intimate with him, but he was always kind to me.

While *Dark City* had been a small-budget, black and white intimate film, *The Greatest Show on Earth* was a Technicolor spectacle with many of the scenes actually shot inside the Ringling Brothers' gigantic tent. Just shooting in Technicolor proved to have its own challenges for Heston. The process demanded the use of powerful arc lights which flooded the scenes and dazzled the actors, especially when working on location in exterior scenes. Heston's blues eyes proved very sensitive to the light and they often became sore and tired. This was actually the only picture Heston made in the old three-strip Technicolor process which required so much artificial lighting, but, as he was to discover, even the single-strip colour films he went on to star in still required powerful arc lamps, irritating his eyes for years to come.

Heston found De Mille to be a director who actually gave his actors very little direction. De Mille believed that an actor should know his job better than anyone else, and gave his performers a pretty free hand in how they interpreted their parts. In fact, much of the direction came straight from the script. Any screenplay for a De Mille film rarely had fewer than four writers collaborating at the same time. They would often spend hours just trying to think up things for the actors to do with their hands so that when De Mille read the script, he wouldn't have to ask, 'And just what is this man supposed to do with his hands while saying that line?'

Heston's job, then, was to study the script thoroughly, get to the set on time and bring to the part that particular chemistry for which he had been hired. De Mille concerned himself more with the technical side, planning his shooting sequences with little models. He'd have his actors come on to the set to shoot a scene which he had meticulously planned and then he'd spend maybe an hour or two making minor adjustments. When the cameras rolled, he expected everything to run smoothly, and if someone didn't do their job right, he'd chew them out there and then. Because of his intricate preparation, he knew exactly what he wanted and captured it all in very few 'takes'. He never improvised or covered any scene extensively, as do many other directors who feel they might just need something extra to add in the editing stage.

For many newcomers to the screen, all this could prove a daunting prospect, but Heston quickly earned the old man's respect and admiration. Heston, however, never did get close enough to the patriarch to call him anything other than 'Mr De Mille'. But then, few did. In any case, he certainly came closer than most, according to Jesse Lasky Junior, one of De Mille's regular writers, who says that Charlton Heston was one of the actors De Mille loved the most.

It was not a particularly physically demanding role for Heston, although some of the other stars (such as Betty Hutton, who had to fly the trapeze) had to get used to calluses on their hands. Heston's only real physical scene was the famous train wreck sequence, shot back on the Paramount sound stages. Eleven extras and technicians were injured in the scene as mock railway carriages turned over and over. The scene called for Heston to lie pinned under bars ripped from an animal's cage. Turnbuckles (devices which enable metal rods or wires to be connected very tightly) were used to twist the wreckage against him, causing a great amount of discomfort.

Just being part of *The Greatest Show on Earth* was quite an experience for Heston, and he seemed to adjust readily to screen acting. At least, it hadn't *seemed* too difficult to him, being young, enthusiastic and excited. It would only be in the years to come as he discovered more about the art that he would find it harder to do.

With the film in the can he had to be patient and wait for the critical and public response to the picture to see if there was still a future in movies for him. At best, the film could establish him as a leading man in pictures; at worst he could go back to New York, which certainly wouldn't hurt.

As it was, *The Greatest Show on Earth*, released in 1952, was a box-office smash and very quickly shot up to second place on *Variety*'s all-time grossers. It also won a Best Picture Academy Award. Charlton Heston, the newcomer, was confident of a chance to make something of his new-found success.

One day De Mille received a letter from a lady who wished to congratulate the director on so skilfully capturing the authentic flavour of the circus, and to express her admiration for Hutton, Wilde and Stewart. In her letter she added, 'I was amazed at how well the circus manager fitted in with the real actors.' To this day, Heston believes that that was the best notice he ever had.

Yet all the attention and immediate film offers that now came were not enough to lure Heston permanently into the Hollywood community. He still had work to do in New York, and so he and Lydia began to commute between coasts, making films in the West and doing theatre in the East.

He had money now. More money than ever before. And he put it to good use. He purchased fourteen hundred acres of timberland around Russell Lake in a remote village called St Helen in Michigan, close to the Canadian border. It was a place he deeply loved, where he could escape to; a place which triggered memories of his happiest boyhood years. It had been his first and happiest home.

He knew he could never really go home again. But he couldn't help trying.

# 2
# St Helen

IN THE ROARING TWENTIES, WHEN PROHIBITION SUPPLIED
the mobsters of America with the highly lucrative and tax-free
sideline of peddling bootleg liquor, Hollywood was in its
heyday, with quick-rich stars hiring their own 'leggers' to
keep the illicit booze flowing. There was nothing the glamorous stars of the silent, silver screen couldn't afford with forty
million Americans queuing up at the picture palaces every
single week, allowing Rudolph Valentino to luxuriate in his
hilltop Spanish-Moorish villa 'Falcon Lair', complete with
black marble floors, while Gloria Swanson revelled in her
golden bathtub and Tom Mix displayed his colourful taste for
interior design with a rainbow-coloured fountain in his
dining room.

The roar of the Twenties was loud and long, and was heard
in every city in the United States where there were folk rich
enough or dangerous enough to make such a sound. But
away from the cities the roar diminished into total silence.

Only the cry of the eagle could be heard above the whisper
of the wind that stroked the north woods of upper Michigan.
This was the domain of the eagles who made their lair
on the point overlooking Russell Lake, untroubled by the
sophistication and civilization of modern America which
was kept at bay by the miles of pine and birch trees, maples
and oaks.

No doubt the eagles had ancestors which had nested there
in the days of the frontiersmen, when the deep, black forests
had covered Michigan before the pine trees were slaughtered
in the process which the professionals called 'lumbering'. The
trees that were there now were second generation, thick and
tall, but the great forests of Michigan were gone.

But there still were some woods there, like a piece of old
Americana which silently welcomed Russell Whitford Carter

and his family as they moved into the tiny community of St Helen, leaving behind the urban hustle and bustle of modern city life in busy Evanston, Illinois.

Russ had landed a job in St Helen as a saw-mill operator, and so he and his wife Lilla had dug up their roots in Evanston to transplant them to Michigan soil, bringing with them their baby son. His name was Charlton, which had been his mother's maiden name. It was something of a strange choice of name, being primarily a surname, and it would in the years to come be the cause of embarrassment for the Carter boy. But in babyhood Charlton was as oblivious to his name as he was to the surroundings in which he was born. His first memories would be of St Helen and the woods and the lakes, but he had been born in Evanston Hospital on 4 October 1923. It had not been a particularly auspicious moment for the world to sit up and take notice of. There was certainly nothing about Russ and Lilla's baby to suggest that he could ever become one of the cinema's most heroic figures or even one of America's finest actors. His veins did not flow with thespian blood. Rather his blood in part had a heritage in the Fraser clan in Scotland.

There were, however, happenings of some significance occurring within the movie world at the time of Charlton's birth. A pioneer of the cinema who had already become a legend in just ten years, namely Cecil B. De Mille, was up to his neck in thousands of miles of exposed film, cutting and joining it with his editor Anne Bauchens, and transforming it into his silent masterpiece, *The Ten Commandments*. Exactly four days after little Charlton's birth, De Mille's beloved mother Beatrice died, never to see the motion picture to which De Mille had devoted himself, and which he would remake a little more than thirty years later.

While Paramount were counting up the exorbitant cost of De Mille's great classic, Metro-Goldwyn-Mayer were preparing to spend an even greater amount on their epic *Ben-Hur*. And almost as Charlton Carter came into the world, silent screen star George Walsh was celebrating his triumph at being cast to play the title-role in *Ben-Hur*. However, by the time cameras started rolling on that film, Ramon Novarro had been re-cast in the role which, in just a little over three

decades' time, would be resurrected for MGM's colossal
sound, colour and widescreen remake.

There was no way that Russell and Lilla Carter could know
that their son Charlton would be the man to personify both
Moses and Ben-Hur more than thirty years later.


It may well have been that Charlton Carter would have
grown into a real city slicker had he been brought up in the
city he was born in, but instead he was planted like a seedling
in the backwoods of St Helen. The seed took root and grew,
blending into the landscape like a veritable young pine-tree.
In a very real sense, Charlton grew out of his environment
into a backwoods hick.

The Carters were no strangers to these woodlands of
Michigan. Charlton's grandfather had lived there since the
beginning of the century, and some of his earliest memories are of sitting on his grandfather's lap listening to the
old man sing 'Silver Threads'. There was also an uncle and
three cousins who were numbered among the population
of St Helen, which at best could boast around maybe a
hundred.

It was an old house that Russ brought his family to live in;
hardly more than a cabin really. And it looked as if it belonged there, smack in the middle of the woods. It was
approachable by a vehicle just one way, along the Highland
Road which was hardly more than a dusty trail. Close by was
Russell Lake which Charlton came to love. It was a joy just to
stand and catch the wind that sometimes drove in off the
north shore. In lakes like this Charlton learned to swim, dog-
paddling in the shallows while his father stayed close by.
Heston recalls of his childhood:

I lived in a very remote part of Michigan, where I attended
a one-room school house. I was one of eleven pupils in
eight grades. I was the only kid in my grade. And it was a
marvellous childhood. A wonderful place for a boy to
grow up. But kind of a lonely way to grow up.

I didn't have any children of my own age to play with.
There weren't enough boys to make up baseball teams or

football teams, and we were more or less thrown on our
own resources.

And so Charlton was a born loner, spending much of his
time fishing or hunting on his own, or running futile trap-
lines that never seemed to catch anything. His dad taught
him to shoot a gun, and together they'd sometimes go driving over the trails and tracks that cut through the woods. He
also had a sister, Lilla, but his most constant companion was a
big German shepherd dog. They went everywhere together,
and Charlton's love of dogs never waned.

With the coming of autumn, the leaves on the maples and
oaks turned and fell, littering the forest floor while the pines
continued to stand tall and rich against the lowering sun.
Then pre-Christmas snow inevitably turned the forest into a
spectacular white wonderland, and Charlton luxuriated in the
experience every year. He welcomed the touch of snowflakes
on his face and he listened as the woods echoed the silence of the
snow swirling about the trees and covering his frozen lake.

A real blizzard quickly built snowbanks against which the
pines stood out stark and ever blacker, and the hill that ran
down from behind the house became the perfect slope down
which to sledge. Dusk brought a whole new dimension to his
woods as the snow thickened and smoothed, giving dim il-
lumination to the darkening wintry forest.

Christmas was a time of traditions in the Carter home – traditions which often prevailed for coming generations.
Christmas Eve would see Charlton traipsing through the
snow in footmarks made by dad, as Russ went in search of a
Christmas tree. Felling a tall pine, Russ would cut the Yuletide tree from the top and chop up the rest for fuel to feed the
log fire which filled the house on Highland Road with
warmth and a cosy flickering glow. Charlton would often sit
in the seat by the window, reading to himself while the smell
of pine needles gently filled his awareness. His imagination
was sparked by the books he read, such as *Call of the Wild* and
*Treasure Island*. Such stories kindled the creative flame in him.
He says:

I used to read books, and then go outside and act them out

by myself. I'd act all the parts in turn. That's probably what started me on the path.

Acting is playing pretend. I was brought up in a very remote part of the country and had no playmates. So I played pretend games with the books I read, as all children do. But I did it more than most. I think that's when I probably planted the seeds that led to the way I'm making my living now.

And so, inspired by Jack London's classic tale of the housedog called Buck who ends up pulling men and sledges over the frozen wastes of the Klondike in search of gold, Charlton would hitch his German shepherd dog to his sledge, and with cries of 'Mush!' he'd go tearing up and down trails through the woods. Until one day a disgruntled neighbour shot the dog and left Charlton on his own again.

With no one but himself for company, he'd take off hunting rabbits, trailing the little furry creatures through the snow for hours, yet never even seeing one. With his nose running and his feet like ice, he'd suddenly become a legendary Indian fighter or a scout in search of food to feed the starving settlers. That was what made life fun, even though he was alone.

One Christmas he actually got the chance to act for the benefit of others when the school put on a play. He landed the role of Santa Claus. He was just five at the time. 'Since it was a one-room schoolhouse with an enrolment of thirteen, landing the role was hardly due to unusual talent on my part,' he says. Nevertheless, he had one whole line of dialogue to himself. He spent most of the time crouching behind a cardboard fireplace, waiting for the moment when he could leap out and cry through his long white beard, 'Merry Christmas!'

Those were the happy years, when Charlton was able to enjoy both the real world about him, for it was a world he cherished with parents whom he loved, and the make-believe world that evolved out of his solitude. He was comfortable with himself and with his environment, and just with the way life was. Outside of his little world, America was in turmoil. As *Variety* put it on 29 October 1919, 'Wall Street Lays An Egg.' Thousands of wealthy Americans became poor overnight. And millions of ordinary folk became unemployed. The great Depression was on. Factories were closing down all over the country. People were being turfed out into the street, jobless, penniless, homeless. The bubble had burst.

But life in St Helen went on pretty much as usual. Russ was an honest, hard-working man and his job was secure. Whatever effect the Depression may have made on the adult members of this small community, it couldn't have touched the young boy who knew his family would never go hungry while there was game to catch in the woods. And there would be plenty of work for dad since America still needed its timber. Life was still simple and sweet, and Charlton's life seemed in no imminent danger of changing for the worse. (Perhaps no change in the life of this backwoods boy would be for the better?) His bubble burst when Russ and Lilla divorced. Charlton was just nine, and his life would never be the same again.

# 3

# Chicago

IN ST HELEN THE WIND CONTINUED TO RUSTLE THE LEAVES, sending a whisper around Russell Lake. The water still lapped gently at the bank, and the distant cry of the eagle echoed above the pines. But Charlton no longer heard any of it. He only heard traffic, horns sounding, a thousand feet stamping the pavement, police car sirens, a million telephones ringing! Such a cacophony almost scared him to death.

Chicago wasn't just a new home. It was a complete culture shock. He had returned to the big city, complete with a new father and an absolute dread of what the future might hold. His mother had remarried in St Helen and the family name now became Heston. Charlton's stepfather was in fact a man whom he had known for some time and had always liked. But with America still in the grip of the Depression the new head of the family was forced to find work at a steel mill in Winnetka, a Chicago suburb.

Charlton was ten. He marks that age as 'a sad, broken time –'

I was very unhappy. It was so remote in Michigan that when I first returned to the city I remember actually being scared to death of the automobile traffic and the noise and everything else that goes with a big city.

I dreaded everything about the change. As a city boy I was an appalling misfit. Literally, I didn't know how to use a telephone, or that I'd better look both ways before crossing a street.

In the woods, I'd not minded playing alone because I was praised for proving my self-reliance. Plunging back into a big city school made me realize the drawbacks of being a loner.

As well as being a social misfit, Charlton also suffered from a lack of height and weight. He was a puny, little kid, easily picked on, as indeed he often was. But as if being an outcast and a weakling weren't bad enough, he was forced to suffer acute embarrassment on his very first day at school in Winnetka.

His teacher was calling the roll. When she came to his name, she called, 'Charlotte Heston.' Young Heston kept his mouth shut as he sank down into his seat, writhing with embarrassment. 'Where's the little Heston girl?' asked the teacher. Heston recalls, 'It was one of the worst experiences of my childhood.'

Life did not improve. Charlton felt trapped, hemmed in by the phrenetic environment about him. The loner instinct in him became more of an affliction. He shrank deeper into his shell and if the world outside seemed to be cutting him off, he was just as eagerly cutting himself off.

One of the very few saving graces of the city was the cinema. He discovered movies and actors. His heroes of the screen were Gary Cooper, Errol Flynn, Hoot Gibson and Ken Maynard. He was intrigued with the whole business of these grown men playing at being cowboys or pirates or soldiers.

But apart from the movies and the books he continued to

read, he still had to cope with the real world, and it was always with relief and gratitude that he welcomed his father's visits. Russ had maintained contact with his children and periodically came to see them. But then, without a word, Russ stopped coming altogether. Charlton waited as the days, weeks and months went by. But there was no word from dad. Not even a letter. He realized that his father had gone for good, and he wanted to know why. But neither his mother nor his stepfather offered any explanation.

He recalls:

It was an extremely traumatic experience. With no warning, my dad was gone. I was ten years old when he walked out of my life without a word. I simply couldn't understand it because we had been so close.

I refuse to play the role of amateur analyst by saying I felt rejected. I was sure he still loved me, in spite of his silence. But I couldn't comprehend it and was unable to get over his disappearance.

It coloured my whole adolescence.

Charlton was not left lacking for love. His stepfather was a good man; a loving husband to Lilla and a caring father to her two children. Charlton admired and respected him, and he grew to love him. In fact, there developed an ideal father–son relationship between stepfather and stepson. And that was very much due to his new father. Whenever he could get off work he took Charlton hunting or fishing, spending time with him and giving him time. He listened intently and sympathetically to the boy's problems.

He was a quieter, more shy man than Russ, but he was stable and well-balanced and tried to inspire Charlton to follow his example. But it was a task for Charlton. He seemed confounded and maladroit. He had accepted his stepfather in place of his dad, but he found it hard to accept that his parents had divorced, and he wanted desperately to deny that it had ever happened. For years he kept his parents' divorce a deep, dark secret and felt a deep sense of personal guilt. As he saw in his teenage years, he was maladjusted, mixed-up, and desperately lonely.

He began attending New Trier High School in Winnetka. It was considered at that time to be the best state-run school in America. But it seemed governed by a whole new set of social rules that contrasted sharply with the simple, backwoods philosophy he had known in St Helen.

He felt totally outclassed by his fellow-students, many of whom came from wealthy families. They wore finer clothes than he; they threw big parties; they drove snazzy cars. He had never even learned how to drive, nor to dance. Yet he was thrust into a life of high school socials where everybody but the wallflowers got on to the dance floor. Charlton just stood to one side on his own, not even daring so much as to make conversation with girls. He was terrified of them. He was looked on as some sort of oddball because he didn't want to conform. But the truth was that he was just too embarrassed to explain that he didn't know how to drive and no one had ever taught him to dance. Whenever he did try to speak up for himself, he simply became tongue-tied. He couldn't even look to his sense of humour to help him through his awkward moments. He hadn't acquired one.

He just didn't seem to belong, although he made some attempts to conform. He agreed to play football for the school, despite the fact that he'd never even seen a football back in Michigan. But he was willing to give it a try. In the process he got his nose broken. Vowing never to play football again, he took up tennis and discovered he could at least hit the ball, and so he pursued this new-found sport.

One sport which he did have success in was shooting. He had always been around guns and could shoot straight. He proved to be one of the best shots in school and made it on to the rifle team. In small but significant ways he was making himself more like the others.

One day he went downtown to see *Twelfth Night*, the first professional play he ever saw. It starred Maurice Evans and Helen Hayes. He was ever more intrigued with this idea of people pretending to be other people. He still played that game, reading books and acting out all the parts himself. Now he saw that other people, grown-ups even, played the same game. He recalls:

I found out that people played these pretend games in organized groups and they were called plays and people came to see them, so it was an okay thing to do. Then I found they did them at the high school I went to, and I suddenly realized make-believe wasn't just something you did by yourself if you had no friends. You could do it with people on a stage, and even take classes in it.

He was hooked. He joined the high school drama class. From that moment on he never wanted to do anything else in life but be an actor.

He certainly had a gift for it which he developed through sheer enthusiasm and determination. It helped also when he virtually grew tall overnight. Until he was fifteen he was the smallest kid in his class, but by the time he was sixteen he had shot up to six foot two inches. He was as skinny as a rake, but he towered over many of his peers, and it enhanced his presence on stage.

He went on to appear in numerous school plays, as well as playing in some productions in small theatres spread around the suburbs, run by various acting groups and clubs. Among these was the Winnetka Drama Club. At last his anti-social shell was chipped away as he engaged in conversations with his fellow-actors who were the people he naturally felt most comfortable with. These were the people who became his friends, but in the world outside he was still ever the loner, and dreadfully shy at meeting strangers. He remained insecure about girls, feeling far too awkward and clumsy around them, and so rather than make a fool of himself he refrained from asking any girl out on a date throughout his entire stay at high school. He concentrated entirely on acting.

He was also proving to be more than just a dumb hick from the country in his academic studies. It must have come as a shock to his peers to discover that he was actually intelligent, and he had his sights set on the Northwestern University of Illinois following his graduation from New Trier.

The spring sunshine hung above the early-morning fog as

Charlton hauled the lawn mower up and down the garden. As long as he needed to earn money to help him through college, and as long as there was someone willing to pay him to do this chore, he would be found mowing lawns most mornings before going to school.

It made for a tiring day. The evenings would see him performing in a school play. By all accounts, the play was terrible. One evening a young student film-maker from Northwestern University came to see it. He was David Bradley who had recently produced and directed a 16mm silent production of *Oliver Twist* and was now engaged in preparing to film Ibsen's *Peer Gynt*, sponsored by the University's School of Speech. He had assembled a large cast of both professional and amateur actors. The fact was that the pros in the picture were out of work and keen to act. However, it came as a blow to Bradley when his leading man, a professional, landed a paying job in summer stock. Now he had to find a replacement, and he came to New Trier High School in the hope that this play might produce a suitable Peer Gynt. He thought the play itself was terrible, but he was struck by a 'gangling, six-foot, startling creature named Heston'. After the performance, Bradley went backstage and introduced himself to Charlton.

'I'm producing and directing a film of Ibsen's *Peer Gynt*, and I was impressed with your performance,' said Bradley.

'Are you a talent scout from Hollywood?' asked Heston excitedly.

'Never mind Hollywood,' said Bradley. 'Would you like to play Peer Gynt?'

Heston agreed, and found himself making his screen debut in 16mm, minus sound. Bradley also had a part in the film as well as co-photographing it in black and white.

He says of Heston, 'I found I had discovered a natural. Heston was not only the rabbit hastily pulled from the hat, but he had a natural presence and instinctive acting ability.'

For a young man shy of the girls, he certainly had his fair share of leading ladies in this, his first, film. He shared one particularly sensuous scene (in which he disguised himself as a prophet, then seduced the girl) with a dark-haired beauty called Rose Andrews. Today Heston views the picture, which runs 85 minutes, as 'a pure, creative film, with wonderful qualities.' He also notes with some humour that he played the whole thing totally unaware that Ibsen had written it as a satire. However, it was not an auspicious movie debut. The film was not seen by the public for another twenty-four years. Heston remains, though, proud of the belief that he is the only successful actor of his generation who ever made both a silent and an underground picture.

David Bradley was not the only one to recognize Heston's talent and potential. The Winnetka Drama Club awarded him a scholarship to attend Northwestern University which boasted one of the best theatrical schools in the country with its Fine Drama Department. Heston had been desperate to get a place there, and he gave a sigh of relief when he knew he would be going there following graduation from New Trier High.

# 4

# Love and War

CHARLTON HESTON MAY HAVE BEEN A 'NATURAL' WHEN HE walked on to a stage, but unless he could rely on dialogue written by William Shakespeare, as a real-life Romeo he was hopeless. He was simply too shy of girls even to feel comfortable with them. Acting allowed him to escape his shy state by hiding behind other personalities, behind beards and false noses, allowing the smell of spirit gum, which he then thought 'the most exciting aroma in the world', to fill his nostrils. But he was plain awkward when it came to handling real life traumas – like dating.

He had just graduated from high school and at last summoned up the courage from down in the depths of his insecure soul to ask a girl out on a date. They took in a show, but he was so nervous and anxious throughout the evening that they were both delighted to say goodbye at the end of their first date. They never had a second, and Charlton made up his mind to concentrate all his energies on his studies in college, and on becoming the actor he'd like to be (a preoccupation which is still with him).

With the summer over, Charlton began attending Northwestern, but still with no transport of his own; he walked each day, allowing the time to be taken up with thoughts of plays and lines and acting. Girls were now the last thing on his mind, and even the war in Europe could not detract from his concentration or his drive to become a professional actor. In that first year at college, he appeared in seven plays and immersed himself completely in the School of Speech course. It's a wonder he was able to keep his eyes open for long enough to read a single script – he was working nights to help pay his way through college and, naturally, spending all day at Northwestern, not only acting but also doing his academic studies.

But neither his enthusiasm nor his physical well-being could be hampered, and he not only survived but positively thrived, spending just about every waking moment with his mind alive with thoughts of acting. He says:

I took a supplementary job for a while, running an elevator at night in an apartment building, and I can recommend that to anyone. It was the best job outside of acting that I ever had, because you can get a little sleep, and I used to rehearse in the lobby. I was on duty from midnight until eight in the morning, you see, and all the people who lived in the apartments were so old that they went to bed very early, so I was left pretty much to myself.

I worked in a steel mill at one time, too, and that was busier. But acting was always the thing I wanted to do, and finally I got to the position where I could make a living doing it. People are always asking actors, and painters and writers too, why they do whatever it is they do, and you can get some very pontifical answers.

But to be honest I have to say I just enjoy pretending to be other people. I think that's what kicks a lot of actors towards this curious career. It's the basic little boy thing of saying, 'look at me, I'm a fireman or an engine driver.' None of us ever quite get over it. It's the kind of kick of being inside somebody else's skin and persuading yourself that it's all really happening. And if you happen to be able to do it so that you can persuade audiences too, that it's all really happening, then they'll pay you for it.

To help him get to the stage where people would pay him, he also took a daytime job doing some local radio work which proved invaluable in his training since the radio relied totally on voice. And so he continued his studies, undaunted in his drive and passion and distracted by nothing and nobody. Nobody, that is, except a pretty brunette who sat in front of him in the drama class.

Lydia Clarke was nineteen and from a small town called Two Rivers in Wisconsin where her father was a high school principal. She was studying drama, but she didn't want to be an actress. Her ambition was to be a lawyer. Previously, Charlton had avoided girls like the plague, but in the acting class he and Lydia were brought into close proximity, and she became the one girl he began to feel comfortable around. It wasn't too long before he realized he was in love with her. She, however, was hardly enamoured of him.

Charlton believes, 'Her first impression of me was that I was the most incredible *creature* on the campus. I probably was.' The *creature* inspired one not-so-kind classmate to observe to Lydia, 'Every family has a skeleton in its cupboard. But the Hestons let theirs out and he wants to be an actor.'

Charlton was unusually courageous in asking Lydia for a date, and at first she resisted: 'When she at last agreed to a date,' recalls Heston, 'things started to look better. She was the first person I told about my parents. Her parents were still living happily together. Yet she listened, and somehow understood.'

But even as the love bug bit, it couldn't chomp a hole big enough for the acting bug to fall through, and Charlton began to infect even the pretty law student, so that eventually they

were both infested with acting bugs. It began quite simply by
Heston insisting that William Shakespeare accompany them
on their dates. 'He took me for a long romantic walk,' says
Lydia, 'and then, instead of making love to me he read *Macbeth*! He got around to the love later.'

So Lydia promptly gave up her ambition to work in the
law courts and set her sights, with his, on working in the
theatre. She was lifted, somehow, by his strong will and utter
determination that he would make it as an actor. He may have
been desperately shy and insecure when it came to dealing
with people, but inside he felt as self-confident about being an
actor as he had ever felt about anything. And this was his
great strength, because while others saw him as a gangling,
anti-social misfit with two left feet, he knew that he had the
guts and the courage to strive for that one goal in life which he
had, and it was this strength which has since overshadowed
the weakness. Lydia recognized it – probably the only one
then who did – and as she says, 'His toughness is not something that grew. He had to start that way.'

'Kids are the most conventional people in the world,' says
Heston. 'It is more important than anything else for them to
conform, and I was always a kind of oddball. So I was driven
into being independent.'

He was realistic too, recognizing the pitfalls of wanting to
be a professional actor. But he wanted it, and was prepared to
go all out to get it. He says:

How could I have imagined at eighteen that I could make a
living as an actor? I certainly had brains enough to know
that you couldn't hope for more than to scratch along. But I
*must* have thought it would work or I wouldn't have done
it.

An actor requires self-confidence because, in Arthur
Miller's marvellous phrase describing a salesman, 'He goes
through life riding on a smile and a shoeshine.' If you go to
read for a part and they say, 'Do you think you can do this?'
you'd better believe you can, because if *you* don't, nobody
will.

He sat alone on the train, his stomach turning at the prospect of coming face to face with Lydia's parents. He still hated to meet people, and he knew that this meeting was important. Now that their romance was something more meaningful than a college crush, Lydia felt it was time he met her folks, and so arrangements were duly made for him to come up and visit during the winter break.

He rode up from Chicago to Wisconsin, and arrived in Two Rivers to find it under a blanket of snow. He found the little narrow house, painted green, where the Clarkes lived. Outside, Lydia, topped by a red woollen hat, shovelled snow from the driveway. She took him inside to meet her parents, and all his anxieties quickly melted away. The cold was left outside as he was warmed by their welcome and made to feel at home. He felt even more at home in the countryside around Two Rivers, and he discovered a lake bordered by rock cliffs that just begged to be explored. He felt a little as if he was back home again, in St Helen, and it felt good to have Lydia with him. They made plans to take a picnic up there one day, when the snow had gone.

But they never did get around to having that picnic. Events in the world around them were invading the lives of Americans everywhere. That winter, on 7 December, the Japanese attacked Pearl Harbor, drawing the United States into the world war.

Still Charlton wanted to be an actor more than anything else. But he was not so unpatriotic nor cowardly as to put his own ambitions before all else. He continued his studies, successfully majoring in Northwestern's Fine Drama Department's School Of Speech, and then, at the age of nineteen, he enlisted in the Air Corps.


Now instead of learning how to be an actor, he was learning a totally new trade – how to operate radios aboard B-25s. He was stationed at Greensboro, way down in North Carolina, several states away from Lydia. They got to see each other only when he was able to get an occasional weekend pass.

He wanted very much to marry Lydia, but she had decided before she even met him that she never wanted to marry.

Feeling he could wear her down, he proposed to her on a weekly basis, but the answer was always 'No', much to his dismay. But he was undaunted. Finally the call came for him to go overseas to the Aleutians. In desperation at the prospect of maybe never seeing her again, he wired one last passionate plea to marry him. He had all but given up hope when a return wire came through reading, 'Have decided to accept your proposal.'

The date was set for 17 March 1944, but it took some careful timing and some last-minute preparation to begin married life. Lydia caught the bus from Illinois right down to Greenboro while he wangled a weekend pass. There had been no time for the usual formalities and invitations. They raced around town, and found an attractive little Methodist church with a minister who was willing to marry them at two hours' notice. There were two ladies arranging flowers in the church. Charlton talked them into acting as witnesses. Lydia chose violet to be wed in, and as the rain teemed down, they ran to the church where the minister and two flower arrangers awaited them. They were duly married, and Lydia had to catch the bus home.

Charlton was next sent up to Selfridge Field in Detroit for his final training before going overseas. Lydia continued at Northwestern, but when it was discovered she was a married woman, she was unceremoniously thrown out of her dormitory. At least they were a little closer now, and most weekends she came to Detroit to be with him. There were just weeks to go before he went off to war, and they tried to make every minute together count. But it was passing by too fast until, finally, their last weekend together arrived.

Hoping for a weekend to remember for the rest of the war, they splashed out and booked a suite at the Book-Cadillac Hotel. The next day was their last together. They wanted to do something special. They chose to go and see Paul Robeson in *Othello*. They needed to check the time the curtain went up, so Charlton went to the phone in their suite to call the theatre. Running his finger down the directory in search of the theatre, he suddenly came across a familiar name – Russell W. Carter. His heart nearly stopped. He hardly dare allow himself to think it but he couldn't help but wonder: 'I think

this may be my father.' He'd always assumed that Russ had
stayed in St Helen but this name was listed under Detroit.
Almost automatically, he began to dial the listed number. Just
in case. A man's voice answered.

'Is this Russell Carter?' asked Charlton hesitantly.

'Yes.'

'Of St Helen?'

The reply was quite casual. 'Yes.'

All Charlton could think to say was, 'This is your son.'

There was a long silence. Then the voice broke the silence.
'Charlton?'

'Yes.'

'Where are you?' cried Russ, his voice shaking. Charlton
told him. 'Wait for me there,' said Russ. 'I'll be right down to
get you.'

It was a highly charged emotional moment when Charlton
opened the door and saw his father standing there, looking
older but still radiating the warm charm Charlton always
remembered. Russ was amazed to see his skinny little son
towering over six feet.

He packed Charlton and Lydia into his car and headed for
his home. As he drove, he explained to Charlton why he had
stopped coming to see him and his sister. He had felt that by
continually coming to visit, he would only cause his children
to suffer. The gulf between him and their mother seemed to
cause an agonizing pull, first one way, then the other, and he
didn't know if Charlton and Lilla could handle it. He decided,
rightly or wrongly, that the only way to deal with it and be
fair to everybody was to step out of their lives completely.

Russ had remarried in 1935. His wife was Velda and they
had a daughter, Katy, so Charlton discovered that he had
another sister. Both Velda and Katy gave Charlton and Lydia
a warm and loving welcome, and from that moment a very
special bond was formed between Charlton and Russ. They
became more than a father and son. They became best
friends, and Charlton came to call him, not dad, but Russ.

Says Heston:

I suppose one reason my father and I have such a close relationship is that we didn't go through the teenage rebel-

lion phase. He missed me, but never guessed how much I missed him. Both of us do realize, though, that his well-meant intentions, when he left his family, were an error.

If parents realized how deeply divorce cuts into the hearts of children, there probably wouldn't be such a frightening divorce rate in the country. Sometimes, I imagine, divorce seems the only sane solution to an unhappy pair. I do think however, it is imperative that, somehow, the natural tie with both parents should not be cut.

Charlton had learned a valuable lesson for his own marriage. But, then, his marriage didn't exactly get a conventional start. The following night they saw *Othello* – and said goodbye.

The next year and a half saw Charlton, now a staff sergeant, serving aboard B-25 bombers in the Aleutians, a series of islands which extends 1,200 miles west-south-west from the Alaskan peninsula towards Siberia. There Charlton and his fellow-airmen as well as soldiers lived in terrible conditions, usually sheltering in just tents or shacks. It's a permanent low-pressure area with cold air blowing down from the Polar regions, hitting warmer air coming up and causing cyclonic conditions from west to east.

While these meteorological phenomena prevailed, the American army and air force fought the Japanese until, finally and tragically, the atom bomb brought the war to an abrupt end in the summer of 1945.

In 1946 Charlton said goodbye to the Eleventh Air Force and, with Lydia, headed East, expecting to take Broadway by storm.

# 5

# New York

THE ONE TAP RAN COLD WATER ONLY. SPACE WAS LIMITED
severely. The rent was forty dollars a month, but the cockroaches came free with the apartment. It didn't look much
better from the outside, situated directly over a shop with
peeling dirty blue paint.

At least here on Forty-fifth Street in New York's aptly
named Hell's Kitchen, Charlton and Lydia could live close to
the theatre district. And that's what counted. To be close to
where the work was. The trouble was, they couldn't find
work, but they weren't despondent.

As Lydia says, 'It was, well, colourful! You don't notice
whether life is hard or not. When you're young you take it in
your stride and enjoy it.'

They were both twenty-two, and excited to be in New
York; to be within walking distance of the casting offices; to
be seen by agents and casting directors, only to be told,
'Don't call us, kid ...' To be almost broke, but not quite
starving. They ate because Lydia managed to get some modelling work. Charlton continued to do the rounds, getting
used to having doors shut in his face. But he never gave up.
He just knew there was a part waiting for him, somewhere,
and so when David Bradley came along with his idea to film
*Macbeth* and offering the star part to Heston, Charlton turned
it down. He did, however, help Bradley to plan the film, as
well as design props and sketch the costumes.

As it happened, it was Lydia's acting career which started
to take off, so Charlton turned to modelling. He was hired by
the Arts Students League to pose nude for the life classes,
earning a dollar and a half per hour, plus free tea and cookies.
Heston recalls with good humour:

In those days male models for art student life studies got to

39

wear little jockstraps. My wife was doing very well as an actress by that time but I had not yet begun, and she made me a little grey velour jockstrap.

While Lydia continued to work at her trade, Charlton continued to be unemployed. He should have been thoroughly demoralized, but he was ever the optimist. He just kept on looking, kept on having more doors shut in his face. He kept himself occupied. He'd drawn for most of his life, and so while Lydia was having success in *Detective Story*, he stayed home sketching. Or sometimes he'd go up to Payne Whitney Hospital where a friend, Jolly West, was a resident in psychiatry, and if he was on the night shift, they'd play some chess.

Jolly West, later to become a noted scientist, was one of a number of friends Charlton had in those struggling years. Those were the ones who remained his close friends through thick and through thin. Most of them were in the same boat; out of work, living in small flats, rearing cockroaches. To them he was Chuck Heston, Chuck being an American corruption of Charlie, and it was the closest they could get to shortening Charlton. At least no one could mistake Chuck for Charlotte!

Charlton and Lydia's first Christmas in that cold-water flat was hardly an extravagant one. They just didn't have the money to buy each other gorgeous presents. But Chuck did manage to scrape up enough money to buy Lydia a green, woollen hat. It wasn't much, but she loved it because *he* had bought it for her.

The New Year finally brought them a break. It wasn't Broadway, but it was acting. The found themselves in Ashville, North Carolina, doing a play at the Thomas Wolfe Memorial Theater. They'd planned just to do the one play, earn a little money and then go back and conquer Broadway, but in Ashville they discovered a completely different attitude towards them as newcomers. Their opinions were listened to and respected, and before they knew it they were co-directors of the Thomas Wolfe Memorial Theater. So there they remained for a while, acting and directing and even doing some teaching. They did six plays in all, including *Kiss and Tell, State of the Union* and their final play there, *The Glass Menagerie*.

They returned to New York in the fall of 1947, full of confidence and optimism that was completely unshakable. Not long after, Charlton managed to get an audition for the prestigious Katharine Cornell Company who were putting on *Antony and Cleopatra* at the Martha Beck Theater on Broadway. He was seen by Guthrie McClintic, Cornell's husband, who was directing the play. In McClintic's office in the RCA Building, Charlton read for the part of Proculeius. He got the part, but not, he feels, because of any particular acting talent he may have displayed.

'I'm sure I got the part,' he says, 'because I'm over six feet tall and Miss Cornell, like most tall woman, likes tall actors around.' Nevertheless, he got the part, and he could hardly wait to get down to the marbled lobby and call Lydia with the news. The play was a spectacular success and ran for seven months, the longest run *Antony and Cleopatra* ever had (generally speaking it is among the more difficult to stage of Shakespeare's plays).

Charlton didn't know it at first, but each night he inflicted pain on Katharine Cornell in the role of Cleopatra. In the scene where he captures her at the monument, he had to bend her over his hip, and each time he did so, his sword hit her hard on the thigh. He was oblivious to this until one evening, arriving for the performance, the stage manager ordered him down to Miss Cornell's dressing-room. He froze for a moment, guessing only that he was about to be fired for something or other. Then he reasoned that she wouldn't fire anyone herself. He began to imagine that maybe she was going to seduce him. He began to sweat.

He arrived at her suite and entered to find her looking gorgeous in a red silk robe. 'Chuck, I want to show you something,' she said. He swallowed hard as she parted her robe and revealed a huge bruise on her thigh. 'Every night when you capture me in the monument scene, your sword hits me. Do you think you could leave it off for that scene?' Heston breathed a sigh of relief, said that he could, and retreated.

When the play finally closed, Chuck was once again an out-of-work actor, and it didn't hurt in the least when television beckoned him.

This was the Golden Age of live television, when plays were performed live for a huge American audience, putting on the actors the same pressures and giving the same fulfilment as did the theatre. But television did not lure the stars of the theatre because it just didn't pay enough and movie stars didn't do TV because they weren't allowed to. Live television, then, relied heavily on new talent, both in acting and directing. There was a whole generation of future film stars and directors who cut their teeth on live TV, and Charlton Heston was among them.

He was cast in a small part in *Julius Caesar*, a production in which the producers were intent on casting only actors who had done Shakespeare on Broadway. That actually limited them somewhat since there wasn't a big name of the theatre who would stoop to doing television, so every name was an unknown like Charlton Heston – they'd done a bit but had not yet become too grand.

During a rehearsal the actor playing Brutus had to retire home with a sore throat. The director called for a volunteer to read the part of Brutus just for the day so they could rehearse the funeral oration scene. Charlton was not one to turn down an opportunity – any opportunity – and he stepped forward to play Brutus for a day.

He followed this with a summer season at the Straw Hat Theater in Mt Gretna, Pennsylvania, and then he was off to Boston over Christmas to understudy the lead in *Leaf and Bough*. Lydia was back in New York working. She sent him a belt that year and they both celebrated the Yuletide apart and alone. The play was due to go on to Broadway, but there was some problem with the leading man. To his delight and surprise the author took Charlton for a drink and said, 'Can you go on in this part tomorrow?' The next day he was the lead, and remained so when they moved to Broadway. It was an important moment for Charlton when he stepped on to the stage of Broadway's Cort Theater, playing the lead role.

But the dizzy heights of stardom on Broadway were short-lived: the play was a flop and closed after three performances.

Five-thirty PM New York Time. The red light goes on.
Charlton Heston launches into the part of Rochester and *Jane
Eyre* goes out live to the East and Midwest. If he blows a line
now, if the director Franklin Schaffner, sitting in the control
booth, switches to the wrong camera, forty million people
will see it on television. Two hours later the West Coast gets
what the trade calls the 'hot line' recording of it. Somewhere
in his Hollywood home, Hal B. Wallis is watching this CBS
Studio One production, and he is particularly impressed with
the tall skinny guy playing Rochester.

For Charlton Heston, Frank Schaffner and the rest of the
cast and crew back in New York, it's an uplifting and gratifying moment when the red light goes off and the play is
through. It's been worth while and there are congratulations
all round. Chuck is particularly pleased. It's the first major
live TV production in which he has played the lead. CBS are
anxious to have him do more, and so he next prepares to play
Heathcliff in *Wuthering Heights*. During the next year and a
half he does a number of other Studio One productions,
including *The Taming of the Shrew*, playing Petruchio, and
*Macbeth*, playing the title role opposite Judith Anderson and
again directed by Schaffner.

It's a heady time for Charlton. The exposure he has been
getting is something he once only dreamed of. And with *Jane
Eyre* he began a long association and friendship with Frank
Schaffner which would result in some of Heston's finest film
work.

He says:

Both of us were, I think, among the fortunate graduates of
the golden age of American television, when the live shows
like Studio One and Playhouse 90 were on and which most
people feel was the high-water mark creatively of television in our country. Frank directed many of these productions, and in a space of sixteen months in New York I
played *Macbeth* and *Wuthering Heights* and *Of Human Bondage* and *Jane Eyre*. That was a remarkable apprenticeship
for a young actor.

Yet for all his enthusiasm and optimism as an apprentice,

he had to release the frustrations that came with the job, and
usually it was Lydia who was at the receiving end. In retrospect, he makes no apology for this. Indeed, Lydia is still the
one who has to put up with his neuroses while he's trying to
work out his problems. But he admits that without her, he
could never have coped with the problems a young struggling actor suffers.

I think that is part of the function of any wife or husband. If
things go wrong, whether you're assembling cars or des-
igning bridges or conducting symphonies or playing
centre forward in a football team, your marriage partner
should be ready to help.
   One of Lydia's prime functions in life has certainly been
assisting me in my work. She's certainly been the central
pivot in my life. She's been there beside me to give me
moral comfort. I don't know how my life or career would
have progressed had I remained single, but it would have
been a lonely, unsatisfying, anxiety-filled sort of life.

# 6

# Hollywood

EVER SINCE CHARLTON HESTON HAD HELPED DAVID BRADLEY
in his preparations to film a silent 16mm version of *Macbeth*,
the two graduates from Northwestern had talked about doing
other Shakespearean films. Movies were by and large a
medium Heston wanted no part of: in 1949 stage actors
looked down on movie actors, and serious actors worked in
New York, not Hollywood. It was a narrow-minded concept
that Heston readily adopted to prove that he was nothing if
not serious. But when it came to the prospect of doing Shakespeare on film, he was interested, even if it was to be one of
Bradley's amateur productions in 16mm. At least their project would have sound this time.

The two most likely titles they would attempt would be *Julius Caesar* or *Hamlet*. Then Laurence Olivier did his *Hamlet* on celluloid, and that settled the matter: *Caesar* it would be. At last Charlton had the chance to play the role he had coveted since he saw Sir Godfrey Tearle play it opposite Cornell's Cleopatra – Mark Antony.

Costing $11,000, *Julius Caesar* is, in the words of Heston, 'one of the most remarkable one-man films I know'. Bradley produced and directed, and he played the crucial part of Brutus as well. Bradley cleverly utilized real buildings for sets, such as Chicago's Museum of Science and Industry which doubled for the Roman Forum. The rest of the cast were from local theatre groups and radio stations in Chicago where Heston returned to just for this non-profit-making enterprise.

Most of the cast tended to look a little small for their costumes. Roman helmets and breastplates just seemed too loose for them, but Heston, though still thin, looked quite magnificent in Roman armour. With that face, he could have stepped straight out of the past. Already, Charlton Heston was beginning to look more comfortable in costume than in twentieth-century clothing.

It was hardly a commercial film and didn't get a general release either in the States or abroad, but it was shown in 1950 at various film festivals and colleges and quickly gained the status of an underground classic. One man who did get to see it was the Paramount producer who had been so impressed with Heston in *Jane Eyre* – Hal B. Wallis. In fact, so impressed was he that he went out to New York, met Heston and offered him a movie contract.

Charlton had not been totally ignored by film studios. In recent months a number of them had approached him with standard studio contracts, hoping to tie him down exclusively to them. But he didn't need that: he wanted to do plays and television. He also recognized, though, that motion pictures could offer him a more secure future, because if an actor made it in films, he could quickly get rich. And being rich was not a prospect that Charlton objected to.

At Wallis's urging, Charlton flew out to LA to meet him and discuss a possible contract. Wallis persuaded a pair of sisters who had been silent screen stars to put Charlton up in their house during his stay, and Charlton acquired the services of a top-notch agent, Herman Citron. Citron succeeded in negotiating with Wallis a non-exclusive contract between him and Heston, allowing Heston to make films for other studios and producers, as well as to do any plays or television he might choose. Wallis was actually something of a progressive producer, who recognized that the old system of movie contracts was dying – he had himself recently allowed his discoveries, Burt Lancaster and Kirk Douglas, to go their own ways. There was now a new breed of actor that refused to be owned lock, stock and barrel, intent on pursuing something more than just a movie star career, and Charlton Heston seemed to be of this ilk. So he became one of the very first actors in Hollywood not to be tied exclusively to any one studio.

A few weeks after the contract was signed, Charlton was on the plane again from New York to Los Angeles. He flew alone, leaving Lydia back East where she was doing a play. He had filled out considerably since making Bradley's *Julius Caesar*. In fact, he was almost pudgy; he would have to watch his weight for the movie cameras, which add it. Since he had broadened, he fought the flab away with daily exercise, and became positively alarmed if his weight hovered much above a respectable 200 pounds.

He landed in LA and was met by Wallis's chief of publicity, Walter Seltzer, who stood at Arrivals checking each incoming face against a photograph he had of Heston. Seltzer was to give Charlton a big build-up even before he made his first professional picture, *Dark City*, which Wallis was personally producing.

Now that he was in town, it was good for him to be *seen*, so Seltzer took him straight to Romanoff's, where Charlton was impressed not by being seen but in seeing Spencer Tracy eating strawberries.

But the life of a film actor didn't prove to be all glamour. Charlton found himself renting an apartment behind Grauman's Chinese Theater, in front of which lay the famous

pavement imprinted with many a movie star's hands or feet.
But behind the theatre, the block where Heston's furnished
flat was situated was more like a bordello. He became increasingly aware of a number of female tenants who seemed to en-
tertain an awful lot of men in their rooms. It was a sad fact
that Hollywood had always been infected with hookers,
many of whom had been young would-be film stars who
never got discovered, but turned to the oldest profession to
make a living.

*Dark City* was made at Paramount Studios, and was typical
of the slick, brooding crime dramas Wallis seemed to special-
ize in. Heston played a con man who becomes the prey of a
man whose brother committed suicide following one of
Heston's cons. The role was a tricky one for Heston as he had
somehow to make this cynical, immoral character sympath-
etic enough to win over an audience. Heston recalls of his
role:

> He is not a very interesting character really, and certainly
> he doesn't show much in the way of convictions. He is only
> mildly disturbed at the sleazy gambling racket he is en-
> gaged in, and finally is a victim, a fugitive trying to escape
> getting killed. Which is fair enough.
>
> That's about all there is to the part. The only point of
> view he had was one of a rootless cynicism. He's sceptical
> because of his war experiences, although that was not
> explored very deeply. I recall this was a point of view I used
> in the part.

Heston's leading lady was Lizabeth Scott, herself a property of Hal Wallis, and promoted by Paramount as a simili-
tude of Lauren Bacall and Veronica Lake. Also in the cast was
Jack Webb as one of Heston's fellow con men. Webb was then
a star on radio with his series *Dragnet* which he later trans-
ferred to the TV screen and so became a rich man.

The director of *Dark City* was William Dieterle, a legendary name in Hollywood with classics such as *The Hunchback
of Notre Dame* with Charles Laughton and *All that Money Can
Buy* to his credit. But he was now past his best and his pictures of the Fifties were generally undistinguished and rou-

48          CHARLTON HESTON

tine. *Dark City* was such a film. As Heston himself notes, 'It's
the kind of film they make on television today and call Movie
Of The Week.'

Upon completion of the film, Walter Seltzer put Heston on
the train and had him going cross-country to promote himself and the film. They hit about twenty cities in less than four
weeks. The gruelling promotional schedule failed to convince the public that *Dark City* was a film they should see, but
it did ignite a closer friendship between Heston and Seltzer
that has endured.

When the summer was over, Charlton decided that it was
time to get back into harness in New York, and he might well
have stayed East if it hadn't been for a chance moment when
his path crossed so fleetingly with Cecil B. De Mille's, and
the great director was impressed with the way young Heston
waved.

Not many months later Charlton was appearing in De
Mille's lavish circus picture, *The Greatest Show on Earth*, and
all of a sudden he found his life was not to be lived out entirely
on the East Coast. He says:

My first film was an unmemorable, although a professionally and efficiently made film. But my second film was the
circus picture which won the Academy Award and was
seen by immense numbers of people. Indeed, it attracted
more critical praise than any film De Mille made. I can't say
what would have happened if the second film hadn't come
when it did, but that secured my place as an important performer long enough for me to get a few turns at the bat.
And that's important. You have to stay in the line-up and
in the first division, and that circus film did it for me.

# Part Two

## 7

# Best Actor

SINCE 1927 MOVIE STARS, TECHNICIANS, WRITERS, DIRECTORS, composers, art directors, supporting actors, producers and other such craftsmen and artists from the movie world had allowed themselves the gruelling annual experience of listening to hear if their names were read out at the Academy Awards ceremony. For those nominated it can be arduous, occasionally humiliating, often ego-massaging. But for everyone that wins, with rare exceptions, it is a moment of supreme glory when they are handed the 13½-inch gold-plated statuette known as the Oscar. For the Oscar is the symbol of the very best in movies, awarded to artists by their peers and in general coveted by anyone who has ever worked in the film industry.

Just to be nominated is an invaluable accolade, but to win one is an unparalleled triumph. And every nominee hoped for that triumph; that's why they always came with a carefully prepared speech . . . just in case.

It was with this kind of preparation, with these thoughts and expectations and hopes, that Charlton Heston found himself in 1960, sitting among the glittering audience, listening to the never-ending list of nominees in each category, followed by the climactic winning name. He had tried not to let it get to him, but it had been a suspenseful six weeks since the day his personal publicist Bill Blowitz had rung to announce that he'd been nominated as Best Actor for *Ben-Hur*. It had been a great feeling just to know he had been nominated, and he knew he had done his very best work in that three-and-a-half-hour epic. But he fought desperately against allowing himself to believe he could actually win the Oscar. He tried not to hunger for it.

Now he sat, his hand wet and tight around Lydia's. It had been a glorious night for *Ben-Hur*, nominated in twelve categories. He felt somewhat shaken with pride each time those involved in the making of the picture who had been nominated, found themselves fighting their way to the stage to collect the little gold man. *Ben-Hur* had been a film to dominate the 1960 Academy Awards, and Chuck could see the film's director, William Wyler, positively beam with the thrill of hearing the title of his blockbuster named seemingly almost every time the winning card was pulled from the sealed envelope.

Best Achievement in Special Effects: A. Arnold Gillespie and Robert MacDonald; with Sound Effects, Milo Lory – *Ben-Hur*.

Best Achievement in Sound: Franklin E. Milton – *Ben-Hur*.

Best Achievement in Film Editing: Ralph E. Winters and John D. Dunning – *Ben-Hur*.

Best Achievement in Costume Design of a Colour Picture: Elizabeth Haffenden – *Ben-Hur*.

Best Achievement in Cinematography of a Colour Picture: Robert L. Surtees – *Ben-Hur*.

Best Achievement in Art Direction of a Colour Picture: William A. Horning and Edward Carfagno; with Set Decoration: Hugh Hunt – *Ben-Hur*.

Best Music Score of a Dramatic or Comedy Picture: Miklos Rozsa – *Ben-Hur*.

Best Performance by an Actor in a Supporting Role: Hugh Griffith – *Ben-Hur*.

It was a blow that *Ben-Hur* had failed to win Best Screenplay, for which it had been nominated, and there were no female performers in *Ben-Hur* nominated. Best Supporting Actress went to Shelley Winters for *The Diary of Anne Frank*, and Best Actress was Simone Signoret for *Room at the Top*.

Susan Hayward, with whom Heston had worked some years earlier in a picture called *The President's Lady* and who was a personal friend of his, came out on to the stage, clutching the envelope in which was the card with the name of one actor on it. Opening the envelope, she removed the card. Perhaps there was something in her face which betrayed the secret before she read the name. But Heston suddenly had the feeling that the name she would read would be his.

She announced the winner.

'Best actor is Charlton Heston for *Ben-Hur.*'


# 8

# The Early Movies

EIGHT YEARS BEFORE HE WON HIS OSCAR, CHARLTON HESTON was torn between two worlds. On the one hand there was the stage and New York where he figured any serious actor had to be – the stage after all, as he has often said, is 'actor's country', and the theatre seemed centralized quite permanently in New York. On the other hand there was Hollywood and movies and much more money – and the chance to become internationally renowned as an actor. He was determined he would not forsake the stage for the screen, but he also wanted what the screen had to offer, which was work, perhaps more security, and – if he struck really lucky – fame, or at least respect and recognition.

The only answer seemed to be to maintain a place in New York and to keep an apartment in Los Angeles. At least they could afford something better than the cold-water flat in Hell's Kitchen, and so that year of 1952 they bought themselves a swish New York apartment. But they didn't see much of it that year – Heston was kept busy in Hollywood.

The move to Hollywood was not one that Lydia welcomed unconditionally. She was concerned about a change in lifestyle and didn't want to sacrifice their own private world for the open-book razzamatazz of tinsel town. She recalls, 'I hated Hollywood at first. But now I realize that half of that hatred was my own insecurity. When you feel insecure you tend to dismiss a place and say it's awful. As I gained self-confidence, I found I didn't dislike it so much.' Most of her anxieties eased when she formed a close friendship with Walter Seltzer's wife, Mickey. Since that time the Hestons and the Seltzers have been the closest of friends.

Paramount were now eager to promote Charlton as a heroic type of actor and prepared a series of westerns for him, the first of which was *The Savage*. He played a white man brought up by the Sioux whose loyalties are torn between the red and the white man. While it offered him very little in the way of a challenging role, it did bring him further needed experience as a movie actor. He was under the eagle eye of director George Marshall who, though not in the league of men like John Ford, was a sure hand at action-packed westerns, and he took the cast and crew out on location to film *The Savage* in the beautiful Black Hills of South Dakota.

In the spring of that year, 1952, the Hestons toured Europe, care of Paramount who wanted him to publicize the De Mille picture. They stopped off in London and there discovered the Dorchester Hotel which they fell in love with and where they celebrated their eighth wedding anniversary. A few weeks later they were in Rome, discovering for the first time the wonders of the Eternal City, one of which was Alfredo's Restaurant where they celebrated another occasion – Lydia's birthday.

They could not have guessed then that they would return to Rome, and Alfredo's, in just a few years' time for what would be Charlton's most prestigious film role.

Back in Hollywood Heston accepted an offer from King Vidor to star opposite Jennifer Jones in *Ruby Gentry*, over at Twentieth Century-Fox. Vidor co-produced and directed this sizzling tale, set in the swamplands of the South. Vidor charged the film with sexuality in the form of the delicious Miss Jones, who played a wench who wreaks revenge on Heston when he jilts her to marry a rich girl. He's only interested in her money, though, hoping to reclaim his family's land. Vidor had previously directed Jones in the torrid *Duel in the Sun*, and he injected many of the illicit elements that had made that grand western such a hit. When Jones has Heston's land flooded, he retaliates by raping her, peculiarly re-igniting their love affair. Heston this time is not so much heroic as proud and scheming, matching Jones's super-siren, causing a few sparks to fly.

Lydia too was making films. In 1952 she starred with Gene Barry in *Atomic City*, directed by Jerry Hopper. Meanwhile Charlton was feeling it was time to 'renew the passport into actor's country', and he went to Bermuda to do *Macbeth*. It was directed by actor Burgess Meredith who had previously directed the film *The Man on the Eiffel Tower* and a number of other plays. Heston found his direction 'highly imaginative', and enjoyed playing what he describes as 'a man-killer part'. In fact, Mark Antony aside perhaps, Macbeth is Heston's favourite Shakespearean role, or possibly even his favourite of any roles. But he has, in playing Macbeth, experienced the dreaded jinx that supposedly strikes every time the play is performed. On this particular occasion he was hit by a motor-cyclist, but his injuries were not sufficient to put him out of the role. In fact, he had never missed a single performance or a day's work in his life, through ill health or any other reason. He wasn't about to let a little thing like being run over stop him now.

Fortunately, Charlton was rarely ill, and when he was it was usually nothing more than a cold. He kept himself fit by constant exercise, usually a daily game of tennis, and if flu did strike while he was working it tended to put him in a sour frame of mind. He couldn't bear for anything to interfere with his work, and lived and worked to a set of stringent standards, making for ever his reputation as one of the most professional people in the business. However, while there were some who lauded his conduct, there were others who took life less seriously and failed to meet the standards he not only set for himself but hoped that others would respect. Similar problems would manifest themselves a little later in his career, but even from those very early days, Charlton Heston was renowned as a stickler for professionalism.

By and large, Charlton Heston was not, in 1952, the kind of actor enthusiastically sought after by major studios as box-office insurance for some of their more ambitious or prestigious productions, and in effect, there wasn't much but routine melodramas or actioners for Heston to choose from. But he wasn't going to be satisfied with being little more than a leading man lending chemistry to a film. He sought for something more challenging to him as an actor, and struck a small vein of gold when Fox had him back to their studio for the first of his historical screen roles – Andrew Jackson in *The President's Lady*, based on Irving Stone's beautiful novel.

It was an exciting role for him to play. 'I think I admire Andrew Jackson more than any of the other men of that genre I've played,' he says.

His leading lady was Susan Hayward who just eight years later would hand Charlton his Best Actor Oscar. But at this time she was a bigger star than he, and her name came first on the credits. She was actually older than him – he was just twenty-nine, she was thirty-five, but still youthful and beautiful. Their chemistry together on screen worked well, and it's sad that they never got to work together again.

To prepare for his role, Heston sought the help of De Mille, who fifteen years earlier had made *The Buccaneer* in which 'Old Hickory' was featured. De Mille made him privy to the research material that his office had collected, and allowed Heston to view the earlier De Mille picture. All this helped him to study the character, setting his own precedent of immersing himself thoroughly in the character of every historical part he would ever play.

As a good-luck piece, De Mille loaned him a wax statuette of Jackson, standing about ten inches high. Throughout the production of *The President's Lady*, Charlton kept the statuette in his dressing-room, returning it when the picture was finished.

The film was part historical, part love story, part adventure. It could so easily have been turned into a lavish spectacle, but instead it succeeded in allowing Heston and Hayward to develop their characters within the modest frame of the film, under the direction of Henry Levin, a prolific, sure-handed craftsman who worked best when restricted by budget on such adventure yarns.

Although not a box-office hit, *The President's Lady* remains one of Heston's favourites of his own pictures (if one can press him enough to admit he has ever been anything like satisfied by any of his pictures). And of his early films, it is still Lydia's favourite.

It was time to return to Paramount and to the westerns they had in mind for him. The first was *Pony Express*, in which he played another real-life hero, though with little historical accuracy – Buffalo Bill Cody. With his long wavy hair flicking up at the back, dressed in buckskins and blasting six-shooters from both hands, Heston made a believable western folk hero. It's a shame that Forrest Tucker, as Wild Bill Hickok, didn't try to at least look as if he was supposed to be wild. But by now Heston had developed his technique of finding his characters through costume and make-up. 'I have to find the outside of the man before I can find the inside,' he says.

He had also learned by this time that there was much to be gained from watching the daily rushes, unlike some actors who won't go near a screening room when the rushes are being viewed by the director. Says Heston:

I want to see the things I do badly. If I see a scene that's good, *that* doesn't teach me anything. You must learn the things you do wrong, and correct them. And in my opinion, an actor must never be satisfied with a performance or even a single scene. If I ever have the feeling that I couldn't better a performance, it'll be time to quit.

Director Jerry Hopper would get used to having Heston viewing the rushes with him. *Pony Express* would be the first of three films they would work on together, Hopper having previously directed Lydia in *Atomic City*.

*Pony Express* has no pretentions; it was a fun film, one of the few such pictures Heston has made. In the opening sequence, Heston waves down a stagecoach when he loses his horse to Indians.

'I'm Buffalo Bill Cody,' he tells the driver.

'Sure,' the driver responds, 'and I'm Wild Bill Hickok!'

'Nope,' says Heston, 'you're not that ugly!'

And so the film pursues this course of friendly ribbing between Heston and Tucker. There are also two women vying for Heston's affections. One was played by Rhonda Fleming, a ravishing redhead who looked quite spectacular in Technicolor, and the other was Jan Sterling, a cool blonde.

The producer, Nat Holt, also helmed Heston's third western for Paramount, *Arrowhead*. Again Heston had a role that was based on an actual person, but this time his name had been changed from the authentic Al Sieber to the fictional Ed Bannon. Chuck found himself back on many of the sets that had been used in *The Savage*, and was again in the company of many of the bit-part players and technicians also from that film. Charles Marquis Warren, who wrote the screenplay for *Pony Express*, also wrote and directed *Arrowhead*. He was something of a specialist in the lore of the American West, and in his opinion Al Sieber was an Indian scout who deserved the Congressional Medal of Honour for performance above and beyond the call of duty.

*Arrowhead* features one of Katy Jurado's earliest appearances in an American film. Previously she had been a columnist in her native Mexico before playing the kind of sensuous, exotic señoritas she was to become famous for. However, in *Arrowhead*, a far grittier, more realistic western than *Pony Express*, she portrays an Indian girl who feigns love for Heston in a bid to spy for nasty Jack Palance as the murderous Apache warrior.

There seemed no let-up in work for Heston in 1953. He found himself on the sound stages of Columbia as a doctor in a mining town in *Bad for Each Other*. Predictably, the film's climax is a mine disaster. It was a dull movie, enlivened by Lizabeth Scott, Chuck's leading lady from *Dark City*. She had been around for several years more than Heston had, but by the time they made *Bad for Each Other*, Miss Scott was on her way out. In fact a year later her career was virtually ruined when a scandal sheet, the infamous *Confidential*, published a feature claiming she preferred women to men, and although she successfully sued them, her career didn't recover.

Heston, meanwhile, continued to struggle with flat scripts and routine adventure films. At least his next picture, *The Naked Jungle*, was a huge hit. Produced by special effects expert George Pal and directed by another special effects wizard Byron Haskin, the film will be for ever remembered as the one with all those million of soldier ants devouring Heston's South American plantation. It's a film which also gave Heston one of his best 'heel' roles which he thoroughly enjoyed doing. But more important, *The Naked Jungle* proved to be his most successful film since *The Greatest Show on Earth* two years before. And two years can be an awfully long time when you're looking for a hit.

Says Heston:

I guess *The Naked Jungle* did turn out quite well. It was a great commercial success, and a fair critical success too. My wife describes the character I played as 'one of those hero-heels you do', and it was the first of them, and is perhaps one of the reasons I was cast in similar roles again. A man who seems to lack understanding, an unempathic man, a stupid man, and yet somehow the audience understand him.

There was a scene in it that a lot of people seem to remember. It's curious because I went to listen to Jimmy Stewart giving a lecture in London, and he made a remarkably valid point. He said that films consist of successful moments. It's very hard to structure an entire performance in the way you can on the stage because you play each scene as it comes along and then you're finished with that scene.

He went on to say that if you play a scene and it works in the final version, then you have in that scene a moment that the audience remembers. And one or two or three good moments will make a memorable film. Half a dozen of them or ten of them can make a great film.

And then he said something that I've found true in my own case with *The Naked Jungle*. He said that people will come up to him and say, 'I saw that picture you made. Can't remember who directed it, can't remember the title or who you played. But there was this scene where you were in a room and this guy turned in the door and you picked up a bottle and looked at him.'

Well, regarding *The Naked Jungle*, that's that kind of film, only people don't say, 'Oh, the ants...' or whatever. But they say, 'I remember that scene where you had this girl, Eleanor Parker, and you threw this bottle of perfume all over her.'

And that's exactly the kind of thing Stewart was talking about, and that's the kind of picture *The Naked Jungle* is.

His next picture, however, was not. *Secret of the Incas* is a totally forgettable film. Again Paramount wanted to exploit Heston in another heel-hero role, this time searching for the fabulous Incan Sunburst among the ruins of the lost Inca civilization. He again found himself among familiar faces on the set: Mel Epstein, the producer, had produced *The Savage*; Jerry Hopper was again the director; many of the technicians were the same as on previous films. By now Heston must have been feeling a little as if he was on a conveyor belt. Heston's co-star, Robert Young, retired from the screen after this film which came at the end of a cycle of undistinguished pictures.

Heston's own career was, in 1954, in the doldrums. He just didn't seem to be going anywhere. At best he was gaining valuable experience by learning his craft inside the rather restrictive confines of the studio system, even though he wasn't totally pinned down to any one studio.

The conveyor belt continued on its seemingly endless way with *The Far Horizons*, the story of Lewis and Clark's expedition into the northwest. As an adventure film, it wasn't at all bad – it came under the directorial eye of Rudy Mate who did this sort of thing all the time – but again the grade of the film was betrayed somewhat by the casting of another actor whose career was floundering – Fred MacMurray. Donna Reed, later Miss Ellie in *Dallas*, also appeared, playing an Indian girl. But for her too it was part of a downward trend, having won that year an Oscar for her performance as Alma, the prostitute in *From Here to Eternity*. Following *Far Horizons* she made just five more pictures and then retired from movies.

Charlton himself must have been wondering at this point if there really was much of a future for him in films, especially when the producers of *Far Horizons*, William H. Pine and William C. Thomas, convinced Paramount to put their boy in their next movie, a trashy soap opera, *Lucy Gallant*. Jane Wyman had the title role, playing a rich woman who, when jilted at the altar, gains the affection of farmer Heston. When her career apparently becomes more important to her than their marriage, he goes off and joins the army and, lo and behold, becomes a hero. By then Lucy Gallant has decided love is more important than money, so she gives it all up for Heston.

It was basically a woman's film, Jane Wyman curiously appealing more to women who love a cry than to men who love a doll. Indeed, Miss Wyman was now forty with Heston a mere thirty-one. But it must have been some light relief for him to note that the part played by Claire Trevor, once again playing a tart with a heart of gold, went by the name of 'Lady Macbeth'.

By now Heston was beginning to feel the need to break out of the mould he had been put in, specializing in heels and rock-jawed heroes. In 1954 he managed to escape movies and Hollywood for a few weeks to play *Mr Roberts* on stage at Palm Beach. It was a refreshing change for him to get back to the theatre where, ultimately, he, the actor, made the play a failure or a success. Film depended too much on too many elements to allow the actor to be anything other than a contributing factor to the final result on the screen.

Returning to Hollywood, he felt the urge to find the kind of movie property that appealed to him as a performer; one in which he could have some say in the final outcome. And he found one at Paramount. It was a screenplay called *The Private War of Major Benson* by William Roberts and Richard Alan Simmons. It was the amusing tale of a tough major who puts his foot in his mouth and finds himself at a Military Academy, training cadets and surrounded by nuns.

Paramount had hoped Cary Grant would play the part of Major Benson, but he passed on it. Heston stepped in and asked to do it, but Paramount couldn't see him, the steel-hard hero of *The Naked Jungle* and *Secret of the Incas*, playing a part tailored for Cary Grant. So *The Private War of Major Benson* was put on the shelf, and Heston must have wondered if maybe his movie career wasn't up there with it.

And maybe it would have been that way if Michelangelo had not looked into the future and used Charlton Heston as his model for his statue of Moses.

# 9

# Barefoot on Mount Sinai

CECIL B. DE MILLE GAZED UP AT THE WHITE MARBLE FIGURE of Moses. It was worth the slight digression in his schedule while in Rome to come to the Church of St Peter in Chains to view first-hand Michelangelo's masterpiece. He looked deep into the eyes of the statue, searching for the soul of the man. He studied the nose that appeared to be broken. He noticed the prominent cheekbones.

Why, thought De Mille, it's just like the fellow who waved!

Ever since the completion of *The Greatest Show on Earth*, De Mille had been planning to remake his silent classic, *The Ten Commandments*, intending it to be the crown of his entire career, dwarfing everything that he had done previously. Taking his idea of retelling the story of Moses to Paramount chiefs Barney Balaban and Frank Y. Freeman, he was given total freedom in the making of the picture. They stipulated only that De mille shoot it in their new wide-screen process, VistaVision.

De Mille took from his archives Jeannie Macpherson's scenario for the silent version which had incorporated a modern parable that made up half of the finished film. Initially De Mille had the same conception for this sound and Technicolor version, but quickly changed his mind, deciding the film would be solely the Bible story. He sent researcher Henry S. Noerdlinger and a team out to Egypt to delve into Egyptian history while cameraman Loyal Griggs was sent to make a filmed survey of the terrain both east and west of the Nile.

In his search for the actor to portray Moses, De Mille studied many photographs of Michelangelo's statue.

Recalls Heston:

During his deliberation in casting the role, somebody

brought to De Mille's attention the startling resemblance between my face and that of Michelangelo's Moses in the Church of St Peter in Chains in Rome. It's true, the resemblance is unmistakable. The nose is broken in the same place. The cheekbones are the same. It's really curious how my face seems to belong to any century but my own.

Heston had been very much on De Mille's mind for the past six months or so, and the director had numerous discussions with him, but hadn't committed himself to anything. Then, as he studied Michelangelo's Moses in Rome, he said, 'Well, if it's good enough for Michelangelo, it's good enough for me.'

Charlton Heston had the role, and in a sense it was quite a revelation. He says:

It was a very gutsy piece of casting on his part. I was very young and didn't have a remarkable film reputation. The only reputation I had was that which was created by the other De Mille picture.

In essence, he put the most expensive picture he'd ever made on my shoulders, and I was not very firmly established. He did have one great advantage. He didn't need a really big name. His own name on a marquee meant as much as any actor's.

Nevertheless, De Mille peppered the film with star names. Yul Brynner, fresh from his Oscar-winning success in *The King and I* was Rameses II, the wicked Pharaoh who would not let the Children of Israel go free; Anne Baxter was Nefretiri, the Egyptian Princess destined to be Queen; Yvonne De Carlo was Sephora, wife of Moses; John Derek was the young Hebrew leader Joshua; Debra Paget was the slave girl Lilia; Nina Foch was Bithiah who drew the infant Moses from the Nile; Edward G. Robinson was Dathan, the Hebrew overseer; Sir Cedric Hardwicke portrayed Sethi I, Moses' adopted father; Martha Scott was Yochabel, Moses' Hebrew mother; Vincent Price was Baka, the Egyptian whom Moses slew; Judith Anderson was Memnet, Bithiah's handmaiden, and John Carradine was Aaron, brother of Moses.

Yet Heston was right. On every poster and advertisement of the film, De Mille's name shone out above the very title of the film.

After what amounted to virtually ten years of preparation and research, with a series of exquisite oil paintings of the major scenes – created by Arnold Friberg – as a unique guide for the set designers and cameraman to follow, De Mille set out for his great adventure in Egypt in October 1954 to begin principal photography on the slopes of Mount Sinai.

There is no Mount Sinai marked on survey maps of the awesome Sinai Peninsula. There is, however, a peak there called Gebel Musa, which means 'Mountain of Moses'. At the base of the Sinai range sits the ancient monastery of St Catherine, where De Mille and his entire unit were permitted to make their base during the filming of the Burning Bush sequence. It was here that the monks had told De Mille's researcher, Henry S. Noerdlinger, that Gebel Musa was indeed the very mountain on which God spoke to Moses.

De Mille wanted to film Charlton walking barefoot over the rocky slopes of Sinai, and a veritable expedition of men, camels and donkeys began a precarious ascent up the towering peak of Gebel Musa. Heston sat atop a billowy camel, as did De Mille. The beasts spat at everyone, and the smell they emitted made Heston feel sick. He hated the creatures, but there was no other way to travel. Finally, the sharp incline was too much even for the animals, and the precious camera equipment had to be unloaded and carried or dragged the rest of the way up. Chuck was only too pleased to climb the rest of the way on foot. His light-sensitive eyes were given a reprieve when it proved impossible to haul the generator, needed to run the powerful arc lights, up the mountain. Instead, Loyal Griggs used only reflectors, capturing a remarkably stark visual effect.

Heston had meticulously prepared himself for the role. He had read a total of twenty-two volumes on the life of Moses, and could recite whole passages of the Old Testament by heart. He had driven Lydia half crazy each breakfast, dinner and supper with talk of nothing but the Dead Sea Scrolls. 'I always conduct a thorough research on the roles I'm asked to play,' he says. 'I like to get under their skins, discover what kind of person they really are.' So, I once asked him, did he get deep enough into the role of Moses to find it in any way a spiritual experience?

He said:

It's very easy to say, 'I walked on Mount Sinai and found God.' I abhor that kind of comment. On the other hand, you can't obviously expose yourself to a man like Moses and remain unmarked. Indeed, you can't walk barefoot on Mount Sinai and be exactly the same. It was certainly an interesting thing to do.

Much of Heston's performance as Moses came, not just from thorough research, but also from the make-up and the clothes he wore. In actual fact, there were eleven different make-ups which followed his progress from a clean-cut Egyptian prince, through a Hebrew slave and shepherd, to the prophet of God and ultimately the aged patriarch with the long white beard at the end of the picture.

Heston has often said, 'I can't play the man from the inside until I know what he looks like on the outside.' How Heston discovered the Moses he played is an interesting example of how an actor like Heston reaches his screen persona. But he doesn't do it alone. In later years he would create his own make-up with the help of his personal make-up artist, Ziggy Geike. In the case of Moses, the actual design of the make-up was by a biblical artist, Arnold Friberg. In fact, the whole look of Moses from head to toe came from Friberg, including the costume.

De Mille had hired Friberg, who admitted he knew nothing about film make-up or costumes, after he saw a series of paintings by Friberg depicting scenes from a book of scriptures called The Book Of Mormon. So enthralled was he with the realism with which the pictures and the characters in them were charged, that De Mille decided to use this artist's talents to create the characters, or the look of them, for his film.

Explains Friberg:

I 'designed' Moses. Not just his costume. It was a total concept of the young prince as he grew into the prophet and
finally into the patriarch. Everybody had thought of him
before as an old, white-haired man. He wasn't. He was a
young man; and later a vigorous middle-aged prophet out
there in the wilderness with a price on his head; a vigorous
leader, a man of God. Well, I had to picture how he would
look. I made a series of pictures showing his make-up
changes, and how he would change in the various parts of
the picture.

He goes up into the mountain and sees the burning bush,
and De Mille said, 'When he comes down I want the audience to know that he has been on holy ground. Something
has happened to this man. We must see it on the screen. He
can never again be the same as before he experienced speaking to the Lord from the burning bush. Now how are we
going to get that across to the audience?'

This was my job. I had to work that out, and the pictures
I did were a guide for the cameraman and the make-up
people and those who did the lighting. I had to conceive of
it all. So I painted these pictures of how Heston should look
at various times, and then they would have costume try-
outs and he would try the costumes on and all that, and
then finally came the day when they made-up Heston completely with not only the costume but the make-up and
everything. Now a change comes over Heston. He
becomes now Moses, and he came walking in and he never
even recognized me. He was now Moses. He was no longer
the Heston I knew. And I had the strange feeling, where
have I seen this man before? Well, I realized he was on my
drawing board. It was the strangest thing to see this thing that
you've created come walking in. It was a little unnerving.

Friberg recalls a story of how his own enthusiasm for the
work resulted in some considerable discomfort for Heston
regarding his wardrobe.

One of the costumes I developed for him was when he was

out there at night tending the sheep under the holy mountain. I gave him a great tawny cloak and I thought we'd
make that out of lion skins. Wouldn't that be great? And
goat hair at the seams. Oh, that looked picturesque and De
Mille liked that so he sent out and he bought three hundred
lion skins.

What I didn't realize was how heavy lion skins are.
Heston's a mighty big boy, but he had a hard time standing
up with this big cloak made of lion skins.

The magnitude of the film really hit home to one and all
when De Mille moved the unit to Beni Youssef, near Cairo,
where the Treasure City of the Pharaohs had been recreated in
intricate detail. It was here that the Exodus sequence was to
be shot.

About 10,000 Arabs were hired to portray the jubilant
Hebrews, starting on their way to the Promised Land. There
were also 15,000 camels, water buffalo, sheep, horses, oxen,
goats, ducks, geese, pigeons, dogs and donkeys. Somewhere
among them were John Derek, Edward G. Robinson, Nina
Foch, Yvonne De Carlo, John Carradine and Charlton
Heston.

De Mille once recalled the awesome experience of Heston
on the set of the Exodus.

Before the big scene, he'd go off by himself for half an hour
in costume, and walk up and down in solitary thought. I
never asked him what he was thinking at those times, but
when he came to the set and walked through the crowd of
Arab extras, their eyes followed him, and they murmured
reverently, 'Moussa! Moussa!' To them, Moslems all, he
was the Prophet Moses.

Heston recalls that experience:

We began shooting in Egypt, and were shooting out in the
desert with literally 10,000 extras. It was kind of a scary
thing because, of course, Moses is a sacred figure to Moslems as well as to Jews and Christians, and it was very odd
to walk through that multitude with the make-up and the

staff, and all you could hear like water in the sand behind you was them saying 'Moussa! Moussa! Moussa!' It was a little scary, really.

To the uninitiated onlooker or perhaps to a less seasoned assistant key grip, the whole set, rambling with extras, none of whom were professional extras – they were hired by the tribe – was a sea of chaos. But not to the master, De Mille, who had been handling movie crowds like this for decades.

He would arrive on the set promptly at 7.30 AM. Co-producer Henry Wilcoxon, who also appeared in the film, was on horseback, giving instructions to the sixty-four assistant directors who mingled with the crowd, carrying walkie-talkies so that De Mille could keep in constant touch with them.

Climbing on to a camera crane, De Mille announced through his gold-plated microphone: 'Ladies and gentlemen, this will be a nation moving – an entire people, its children, its aged, its goods and livestock. If you have prepared well this will be the awe-inspiring event that it is in the Bible and in history.'

Yet still he was not ready to roll the cameras.

Says Heston:

Instead, he just sat there hour after hour in the blazing sun with his binoculars clamped to his eyes. He'd keep shouting things like, 'The woman with the blue shawl behind the feet of the third colossus from the back. I don't want her there. No, no. The *third* colossus. That's the woman. I want her down on the sand.'

I kept thinking, 'If he does this with every one of those 10,000 people, we will never, never turn a camera.'

It was five hours before De Mille finally blew his little gold whistle to commence the shooting.

The Exodus sequence took days to capture on film. It very nearly didn't get completed. De Mille suffered a heart attack after climbing a 107-foot ladder to reach a camera platform perched on top of the city's gates. Determined to reach the ground under his own power, he climbed all the way back down again. He was bundled into his car and driven to Cairo. His doctor ordered him to bed under an oxygen tent for at least two weeks and then to remain in an ordinary bed for a much longer period. The doctor told him that for him the filming was over. De Mille refused to stay in bed and spent all night on his knees in prayer.

Heston recalled, 'It happened on a Friday, and, by God, he was back on the set on Monday. It was just incredible to see how he could have done it. But he did. And the bulk of the film was still ahead of him.' One can't help but wonder if De Mille received some form of intervention from a source higher even than Paramount Studios!

It was during this period of filming that news came through to Charlton that the screenplay of *The Private War of Major Benson* had been sold by Paramount to Universal. Heston immediately cabled Herman Citron, telling him he had to have that property at any cost. Citron succeeded, promising Universal that Heston would make the film for a percentage of the profits and no salary.

Before they left Egypt some celebration took place among the Arabs, and Charlton duly joined in. He later wished he hadn't when he was offered the eyeball of a sheep to eat, stuck on the point of a Bedouin's spear. Not wishing to offend the host, Chuck munched away on the eye displaying even more courage than he would show on the screen.

By the end of November 1954 the unit was back in Hollywood, filming on vast sound stages at Paramount Studios. Lydia was now six months pregnant. It was a joyous time for the Hestons, who'd longed to have a baby.

In the meantime Charlton still had the task of getting those tablets of stone down from Mount Sinai, now constructed on a sound stage. While Heston is up on the mount watching 'the finger of God' blasting the ten commandments into the side of Sinai, the children of Israel, according to the script, were revelling in a drunken orgy around the golden calf.

Says Heston wryly:

They'd been doing an orgy scene for days, with girls rolling around in the grapes in orgiastic frenzy, and this one tired girl really did say to the assistant director, 'Hey

Eddie, who do you have to sleep with to get *out* of this picture?'

Anyway, we finally come to the scene – obviously I've been absent from all these revelries – in which Moses appears in a cloud of nebula on the top of the mountain, with the tablets in his hands, and says, 'Who is on the Lord's side? Let him come to me,' and everyone cowers back.

Well, we just got that bit in when someone yelled 'Lunch!' I started back to my dressing-room where I always ate alone, still trailing clouds of Mosaic glory behind me, when I passed one of these little slave girls who'd been slaving away in the orgy for days, and she said to me, 'Party pooper!'

Charlton's final contribution to the film was to supply the voice of the Lord for the scenes of the burning bush and the giving of the commandments. So Charlton Heston really has played just about everyone from God down.

With his portrayal of Moses in the can, he went virtually straight into *The Private War of Major Benson*, barely giving himself time to allow the Moses persona to drift away. (He can never leap straight into a role in a film, because it takes a little time to 'find' the man he's playing, and that means that during the first days of shooting he sometimes feels his performance to be weak.)

*Major Benson* was Chuck's baby. He was responsible for getting the film set up, with the help of Herman Citron, but at least he didn't have the worry of being financially involved. Universal paid the budget as controlled by producer Howard Pine. Jerry Hopper was again Heston's director, undoubtedly a safe choice. Charlton had some authority in the casting, which was restricted somewhat by budget. However, talent was more important than star names, and so Julie Adams, a leading lady of supporting features, became his leading lady. Many of the cast were children and juveniles. Of these, seventeen-year-old Sal Mineo became a star in his own right.

Heston loved the film's script, and he loved playing it. It was a rare opportunity to try his hand at comedy. He did very well in it too: it proved to be an entertaining movie, and Heston did well with the comedic dialogue.

He says:

Comedy is about the only genre I haven't explored much. I would be glad to do more comedy roles, but the trouble is Jack Lemmon gets all the good parts. Whenever I get a comedy script, they've got Jack Lemmon's fingerprints all over it. He's already read it and thought it not very good.

It's ironic in a way that Heston's first comedy should be one that was tailored for Cary Grant. He says:

When I began training to be an actor, Cary Grant was at the height of his remarkable career, and I always thought in a sense it would be marvellous to stand around in beautiful rooms, saying beautiful things and wearing beautiful clothes and talking to beautiful women. But I think nobody ever did that better than Cary Grant.

With or without Cary Grant, *The Private War of Major Benson* was a commercial success, and with Charlton earning a percentage of the net, it helped to pay his bills for some years to come.

During the filming of it, Lydia gave birth to a baby boy on 12 February 1955. With the pride of parenthood mingling with Charlton's pride in his Scottish ancestry, they named him Fraser – Fray for short.

At that time De Mille was still hard at work on *The Ten Commandments*, mainly in editing the film and supervising the special effects. He still had the scenes of the infant Moses to shoot, and having known that Lydia was expecting a child, he'd decided to hold on until after the birth in the hope that the infant Heston would be willing to make its movie debut for his mighty epic.

Fray was three months old before Charlton gave his consent, but Lydia was not at all sure about it. She says:

I had heart failure because he was cooped up in that basket

and I thought he'd suffocate. But, of course, there are very strict laws about how long they are allowed to work.

It was supposed to be just for fun, but it turned out anything but. There was our one and only child, after ten years of waiting, floating down the Nile in a basket. Chuck was standing in a tank that represented the river. He picked Fraser up, felt him and thought, 'That's just baby wet,' and didn't pay any attention to it. All of a sudden the basket went down.

Cecil B. De Mille came rushing over, crying, 'It's all right. The Bible says, "And the babe wept."' By crikey, the babe did, too!

Editing *The Ten Commandments* was a mammoth undertaking for De Mille and his editor, Annie Bauchens, and it was more than a year later before Heston finally got to see the finished movie at a private screening hosted by De Mille. Heston was excited and moved by what he saw up on the screen. He recognized the flaws in it, but knew too that De Mille was the only man who could have captured the pure magnificence that was up on the screen. Typically, he was dissatisfied with his own performance, and he was also disappointed with the special effects.

He says:

It was an enormous role, but like Christ it is unplayable really. It was beyond my capacities then, and it would be beyond my capacities now. I could do a better job now than I could then, but any actor with the brains God gave geese would be able to say that about any role.

The Exodus is the best thing in *The Ten Commandments*. It's quite moving. A marvellously exciting experience, because there are all those people, and they really are moving. You're prepared to believe they're going to walk to the Promised Land.

Certainly the Red Sea sequence is not as good as the Exodus, in my view, either structurally or in its final result. You cannot put aside any consideration of the technical qualities of the process work because a scene like that really either works or it doesn't. It requires belief. You have to believe it, and the technical solution to the parting of the sea is what makes the scene stand or fall. I suppose now it could be done better.

De Mille was ecstatic about Heston's performance, despite whatever misgivings Heston himself might have had. Stated De Mille, 'Charlton Heston brought to the role a rapidly maturing skill as an actor and an earnest understanding of the human and spiritual quality of Moses.'

De Mille previewed the film in the Mormon capital Salt Lake City where the audience responded with overwhelming enthusiasm. The critics were, perhaps, not quite so kind in their appraisal of the film, but that didn't matter. What counted for De Mille was that *The Ten Commandments* drew praise from countless religious leaders, and it was these reviews which Paramount sold the film with.

The picture opened triumphantly at the Criterion Theater in New York on 8 November 1956, and then at the Stanley Warner Theater in Los Angeles six days later. It was an unqualified hit, registering huge box-office earnings. Its success meant different things to De Mille and Heston. For De Mille it was his last and greatest success. He made the film literally for no personal salary. In essence, the picture was a message that he believed in personally, and he wanted to give it to the world as a gift. For Heston, it shoved him right up out of the routine action hero mould. He was a star, or in his own preferred words, 'a public actor'. It came at a critical point in his career, and it did everything he hoped it would.

He says: 'Ultimately, *The Ten Commandments* will have been seen by more people than any other film I have ever made, or probably will ever make. If you can't make a career out of two De Mille pictures, well I guess you'll never make it.'

# 10

# A Touch of Genius

CHARLTON HESTON MOVED HIS HORSE CLOSER IN, THE LASSO loose in his hand. He dropped the loop over the cow's head and pulled tight. The cow didn't flinch. Heston wasn't surprised, really. The cow was, after all, just a dummy. But Frank Cordell, the Hollywood cowboy, would give Heston the chance to rope a real cow in a few days. He had to get the technique right first.

Chuck had played in westerns before, but he'd never had to rope a cow yet. In preparation for *Three Violent People*, in which he played a rancher, he'd need to know how to do something as basically cowboyish as rope a cow. He knew the value of this kind of training prior to the start of filming because, once the cameras were rolling, there wasn't time to pick up such skills.

Hal Wallis had just sold his contract with Heston to Paramount so now he was working for the studio, though he still had the contractual independence to make films elsewhere. But he was committed to make two more movies for Paramount, and *Three Violent People* not only had a good script by James Edward Grant but would also help him to work off his contract with one film to go.

The three protagonists of the title were the rancher, played by Heston, his wife who was once a prostitute, and the rancher's one-armed brother who wants to kill Heston. Neither character is totally wholesome. Heston is a heel again. Indeed, the film isn't too unlike *The Naked Jungle*, only this time he doesn't have soldier ants threatening his land: he's got a vengeful brother.

To play the wife, Paramount wanted Anne Baxter so that she and Heston could recreate some of that screen chemistry that in small part contributed to the romantic element of *The Ten Commandments*. Actually, Baxter and Heston never really did hit it off away from the set, but they worked well together. 'We never had a cross word, but I did not find her enormously warming and there was no great personal stirring between us as friends,' Heston told me.

He wasn't too happy about the casting of the brother. Paramount wanted Tom Tryon, a newcomer who'd been a production assistant on television before switching to acting. Charlton had many misgivings about the choice of Tryon who did not seem to be a strong enough actor to carry off the vital role of the brother. Heston began to flex his movie muscle a little, now that he was feeling that at last he had some say in the casting of his films, but Paramount were adamant, and Tryon was cast.

Director Rudy Mate took the cast through a pre-production rehearsal period, most unusual in movies. As shooting commenced, Heston began to feel more confident about the choice of Tryon. Ultimately, Tryon was very good in the part and proved quite essential to the finished film because it relied so much on the performances of all three actors.

When Heston saw the picture he realized just how wrong he had been about Tryon who, after that, became an actor of some prominence before he switched from acting to writing novels and screenplays, as well as producing his own pictures.

In the summer of that year, 1956, Charlton and Lydia returned to the stage to do *Detective Story*. Charlton had long wanted to wrestle with the lead role of that play, and especially to do it with Lydia, who had played her part before. It was actually a stock tour, playing four engagements with Charlton and Lydia and two or three other key actors taking the show on the road, casting the smaller roles with actors from whatever locations they played in.

Before embarking on the gruelling tour, they spent two weeks at their lodge in St Helen, around Russell Lake. Charlton's beloved piece of land was now under protection by the government from being developed. It was a haven to which he could escape and lose himself in memories of his childhood, in the days when he really was happy.

*Detective Story* opened at Newport, Rhode Island with

some success and then moved to Fayetteville, New York where the play went even better. Heston loved the part of McLeod, and felt himself growing into the role with each performance. He always felt a certain power on the stage that never came with film, and he revelled simply in being an actor in the theatre again.

He says of the theatre:

In theatre, the stage is, finally, actor's country. No matter how gifted the director, no matter how much he gives you, when the curtain goes up each night, the actor must begin at the beginning. It's like building a sandcastle on the beach. You make it complete, perfect, and the tide comes in and it's gone.

In a film the actors do their best. Whatever gift they have, they bring to it. Whatever contributions they can make, they make. Whatever controls they have on the script or the casting, they exercise. But when the shooting is finished, the actors go home.

There is no movie, just five thousand little rolls of film with little rubber bands around them in the cutting room, and then the director and the editor sit down and make a movie.

Throughout my career I've switched from one medium to the other, and found each rewarding. Each has its challenges. I certainly am not one of those actors who disdains film as the medium where he makes his living and finds the only pure art to be sought is on the stage. I don't think that at all.

So for different reasons I like acting in both mediums.

After the success of *Detective Story* at Newport, he returned there with *Mr Roberts*, his own choice of play which he considers possibly the best of that genre. Putting it all together was a rush job which leached some of the pleasure out of doing it. Nevertheless, it was another success and prompted the City Center in New York to ask him to bring the play to them.

Prior to this engagement, he starred in *Forbidden Area*, a live telecast for Playhouse 90 which disappointed him. It was not a happy performance for him. He'd caught a cold, just about the only illness he ever suffered from, and he had to fight it all the way through the broadcast.

Looking forward to something more rewarding at the City Center, he arrived in New York expecting to be reunited with his previous *Mr Roberts* director Mike Howard. Instead he found Johnny Forsythe, who had himself played Heston's part on Broadway. Since he had approval on the director, Heston made loud noises to Joshua Logan, the creator of the play, threatening to leave the play altogether.

He finally decided to let the matter drop and got on with the work at hand. He also had the chance to work a little with Logan himself, an invaluable experience for Heston who was able to discover some weak points in his own concept of Roberts and so correct them. In working with Forsythe, Chuck steered clear of anything that might make them clash over a part they had both played, and they succeeded in collaborating on what amounted to a critical and a commercial success.

The swirling snow enveloped Charlton as he paced off from the car into the night in search of the road that led to St Helen. They'd already fought their way through blizzards and up snowy hills, and as familiar as he was with the territory, Charlton couldn't see more than ten yards ahead.

Discovering the road that lay somewhere under the deepening blanket of snow, he traipsed back to the car and took the wheel. They arrived at the lodge that night, and two days later it was Christmas, spent with Russ and Velda, and summoning up all the familiar recollections of Christmas as a boy in the woods he loved so much.

Over the holiday period, Charlton read through a pile of scripts. He was more than ever in demand now, but the quality of the stuff he ploughed through didn't exactly excite him. There was one, however, which seemed promising. It was *Touch of Evil* from Universal who wanted him to play a Mexican detective. It was a fairly routine thriller – little more than a superior B-script really.

He called Universal on the phone and asked who was going to direct.

'We've not set anyone to direct yet,' they told him. 'But we have got Orson Welles as the crooked cop.'

'Why not have him direct too,' suggested Heston.

'You're kidding,' they said.

Heston wasn't. One of his favourite films was *Citizen Kane*, which Welles had written, directed and starred in back in 1941.

The suggestion was put to producer Albert Zugsmith who was keen on having Heston in his film. He and Universal decided that rather than have Heston back out – he was now riding high on the wave of success that *The Ten Commandments* was reaping – they'd better ask Welles to direct.

With Welles secured as the bait, Universal hooked Heston for the film with no up-front salary, but a deal to pay him 7½ per cent of the gross. Charlton was now wildly enthusiastic to do the film for no other reason than the fact that Orson Welles was directing it *and* rewriting the script.

Welles's finished screenplay sent a wave of panic through Universal. His rewrite job had transformed the predictable melodrama that they had envisioned into an offbeat cop film. Charlton, however, was enthused by what he read, and even more so by Welles's idea to rehearse the entire film through at his house. In the process, Charlton felt himself growing as an actor, absorbing everything that Welles threw at him as both director and actor. Says Heston:

It was a remarkable learning experience for me – one of the most valuable in my whole film career. I probably learned more about acting from Welles than from any other director. He is himself an actor, and an incredibly resourceful communicator. He understands actors and he can communicate with them. He did so to me in great detail, and very valuably.

Heston's only criticism of Welles was that he seemed to feel the need to conceal from Heston the fact that the central role was the one he played himself while Heston's part was secondary. As writer and director, Welles added a couple of scenes specifically for Heston which were unnecessary.

Heston really discovered what an innovative director

Welles could be on the first day of shooting. Welles had them rehearse all day and didn't begin filming until 5.45 PM, by which time producer Zugsmith was turning pale at the thought of going over budget and over schedule on the very first day. But two hours later Welles cried, 'Cut! Print! That's a wrap on this set.' They were suddenly two days ahead of schedule, with some dozen pages of shooting script all on film which were to have taken the next couple of days to complete.

The famous opening sequence was shot in a single night. Welles did the whole thing in one continuous take, following Heston for three blocks while the dialogue continued, culminating in Heston kissing his leading lady, Janet Leigh, followed by a car exploding – all in probably the longest single tracking shot on record.

Every day Heston was amazed by some innovative technique or other, even to the point of transposing dialogue from one set to a completely different one. Charlton felt so much that *Touch of Evil* would turn out to be a superior picture.

Even in dubbing dialogue, Welles proved to be a wizard. Heston found himself dubbing in completely new dialogue over one scene, creating a new climax. From that time on, Charlton has made creative use of the dubbing, or 'looping', sessions to improve on a performance more than he would have ever thought possible.

Universal, however, were not as impressed with Welles as Heston was. The film was just too far ahead of its time. The story was there on the screen, but Welles didn't spell everything out for the audience – they had to work a little harder to follow the film. Audiences today have no problem doing this, but in 1957 if a man went from A to B in a car, you had to *see* him in the car, rather than just arrive suddenly at B. So Universal set another director, Harry Keller, to shoot additional orienting footage and refused to allow Welles to set foot back on the set. Initially, Heston refused to work on the new stuff without Welles on the set, but, as his lawyer pointed out, he was legally bound and had to comply. In the process, though, Heston held up the filming for one day while he tried to untangle the legal and moral wrangle he found himself in, but he reimbursed the studio for the lost day, costing him some $8,000 out of his own pocket.

Considering his excitement and enthusiasm during production and his regard for Welles, it's surprising to note that when Heston first saw *Touch of Evil*, he was greatly disappointed. In fact, it's a point that today surprises even him. He says:

> The film is perhaps not a great film. It's not the equal of Welles's *Citizen Kane*. But *Touch of Evil* is certainly a worthwhile film with a great many virtues and one, I think, any film maker would have been glad to have been part of. And why I didn't recognize that when I saw the finished film for the first time, I don't know! Perhaps I had expected more. Perhaps I expected it to be the incredible project it seemed to us while we were doing it.
>
> Contrary to legend, there is no 'lost Welles version'. The picture is very close, I think, to what it would have been if the studio had let Orson stay on it until the final dub.
>
> I must say that it was a marvellous experience to work with arguably the most talented man in theatre and films in our time. That doesn't mean he was the best actor or the best director. But whatever talent is – which is just a word we tack on the intangible contribution in artists that we can't measure in other terms – Orson had it. And again, *Touch of Evil* is certainly not a great film, but it has been described as the best B-movie ever made.
>
> To Welles I'd attribute that over-worked word – genius!

*Touch of Evil* was neither a critical nor a commercial success. It has, however, become something of a classic over the years and is today considered by critics and movie buffs alike to be one of Welles's finest films. As Heston says, '*Touch of Evil* is not *Citizen Kane*, but it has been placed not far behind *Kane* in the list of Welles's films.'

Despite Charlton's initial luke-warm reaction to the film, he wanted very much to work with Welles again, and they discussed a number of subjects, among them *Julius Caesar* and a film version of a science fiction book called *I Am Legend*. But Charlton found he never could button Welles down long enough to get any project off the ground. 'Unfortunately, Welles is inclined to be undisciplined, careless perhaps, and often misguided,' he says.

But even if he never got anything else out of his working relationship with Welles – and he certainly didn't get much of a financial return – he recalls his experiences of working with Welles as among his most memorable, and always cites Welles as one of his very favourite movie directors.


# 11

# The Wyler Touch


JACK L. WARNER TOOK ANOTHER LOOK AT THE CONTRACT HE'D signed for Heston to do *Darby's Rangers*, with William Wellman directing.

Herman Citron, dubbed 'The Iceman', had made the terms perfectly clear. Heston now worked for a percentage of the profits. Universal had agreed to those terms for *A Touch of Evil*, and so had Warner Brothers for *Darby's Rangers*. But Jack Warner hadn't quite realized just what it had meant. After all, few actors then ever worked for a piece of the gross.

Yet there it was in black and white. Heston was to receive his share of the movie's profits. Jack Warner made a hasty decision. He promptly fired Heston and cast a contract player in the role – James Garner. Equally promptly, Heston sued.

In court Charlton gave a calm, if somewhat wordy, deposition. There had been a time in his life when he rarely spoke. Now he had a tendency to over-state. After his deposition, his lawyer advised him, 'You know, Mr Heston, it's perfectly okay to answer questions with a simple yes or no.'

Jack Warner, however, said too much. His anger came quickly to the surface when questioned, and he blurted out, 'All them damned actors deserve anything lousy that happens to them.' That settled the matter as far as the court was concerned. They ruled in Heston's favour, and he was awarded a settlement from Warner Brothers that provided the initial finance he needed to go ahead and start looking for a house of their own at long last.


That dreaded red light came on and once more Heston was telecast live to the nation. This time he was doing *The Anderson Court-Martial*, complete with stuck-on moustache. It was, he felt, a superb script and the best part he'd had in some time. He was delighted with Ralph Nelson's direction, and apart from the moustache nearly falling off in front of forty million viewers, the play ran well, satisfying his actor's ego enough to allow him to take a drop in billing for his next picture, William Wyler's *The Big Country*.

He didn't particularly like his role, playing a heavy for the first time, and it was really just a major supporting role. He had accepted it only because he didn't want to pass up the opportunity of working for Wyler. It wasn't the happiest of films to make. Its star, Gregory Peck, was also co-producing with Wyler. They came into conflict as producers, and then carried this over on to the set in their actor-director relationship. Wyler, being who he was, usually got it his way.

He never let up on his actors or a scene until he was convinced that he had got all he could out of them and the script. He might make a dozen or more takes on any one shot, exploring every angle, concept, motivation and wringing every last drop of emotion from it. This was a technique Heston was unused to – he tended to want to get on with things. He had to learn to be patient and rely on Wyler's instincts which, after all, had been proven over a period of more than three decades.

Charlton learned not to expect praise from his director. Wyler simply explained to him, 'Look, if I don't say anything after a take, that means it's okay.'

Just a single scene under Wyler's direction could be a gruelling experience. He had Peck and Heston shoot a fist-fight sequence from morning till evening, by which time both actors were utterly exhausted – which suited the scene well.

Even the women came in for some rough treatment. When

Charlton Heston towers over his leading lady, Susan Hayward, and best-
selling historical novelist Irving Stone, author of *The President's Lady*. In the
1953 adaptation of the novel, Heston played his first US President, Andrew
Jackson.

Heston – eagle-eyed with Fred MacMurray in *The Far Horizons* (1955), and impassive in *The Ten Commandments* (1956) with Vincent Price, Sir Cedric Hardwicke and Yul Brynner.

*The Ten Commandments* established Heston as an epic figure. His authoritative Moses dominated the film.

*Ben Hur* (1959): two moments with Messala (Stephen Boyd), the Judaean prince's best friend who becomes a deadly rival.

Heston and Carroll Baker had an on-screen tussle, Carroll ended up with bruised wrists from Chuck's big grappling hands.

Explains Heston:

Willy had us do that scene over and over again before he was satisfied. He kept urging her to break loose while insisting I mustn't let her go, and by the end I'd hurt her wrists. The poor girl was in quite a state at the end of it.

And here's another insistence on getting just what he wants. Out in Rome, six months after we'd completed *The Big Country* in the States, he had me do a special close-up to be slipped in the big fight scene I have with Gregory Peck. Ironically, he didn't use it in the end.

Charlton's estimate of leading ladies, which had not always been high, rose dramatically during his scenes with Jean Simmons. Of female stars in general he once said,

Some of them are very unprofessional in their attitude. They don't care very much about what they're doing. They're too disenchanted by the movie-star bit, and tend to regard it as a social engagement. The industry has created its own monsters, and some of them are feminine.

That was his attitude then, and it hasn't changed too much over the years. However, he continues:

Among the ladies of my profession I highly respect is Jean Simmons. Not only is she extremely gifted, but what I find even more praiseworthy is the fact that she's managed to remain unaffected by the corrosive influences and the pitfalls of fame that have destroyed so many of her sister-actresses.

In all, filming *The Big Country* took Heston, even with such a relatively small part, three months of hard toil and sweat to accomplish. But he was glad that he came to the decision to work with Wyler, and in retrospect it was one of the best moves he ever made because just about at that time

MGM were in the process of persuading Wyler to direct their mammoth remake of *Ben-Hur*.


To Charlton, it was like giving his wife the best Christmas present ever. He stood by her side on the mountain, looking out over the canyon, allowing her to take in the same breathtaking view that had captivated him. Below was Hollywood, close at hand and yet simultaneously far removed. And beyond they could see the Pacific Ocean. Russ had found it first; an eagle's eye view of the canyon, just begging for someone to come along and build a house there. Chuck loved it the minute he set eyes on it and was eager to have Lydia give her approval. When she saw it, she just stood there, speechless. She drank in the beauty before her, and tears began to flow.

Charlton was thunderstruck. 'What's the matter?' he cried. 'Don't you like it?'

Recalls Lydia, 'In spite of his size, he looked so much like an anxious little boy that I had to laugh instead.'

So the plot of land was purchased, and the Hestons started making plans to have their house designed and built.

Heston was working on another small film role, but this time it was more of a cameo. He was again portraying Andrew Jackson in the De Mille production, *The Buccaneer*. This time De Mille was not directing. He had originally planned to make this a musical version with Yul Brynner as Jean Lafitte, but Brynner was dissatisfied with the material and the treatment, and De Mille eventually decided it would be a straight remake of his earlier swashbuckler. By this time, however, he was not up to directing the picture and sought someone else to fulfil the task.

One day he was having lunch when his daughter, Katherine, and her husband, Anthony Quinn, came by. De Mille asked Quinn if he thought Budd Boetticher might be a good choice to direct *The Buccaneer*.

'He's not your kind of director,' replied Quinn.

Suddenly De Mille leaned forward and said, 'Tony, how would *you* like to direct it?'

Quinn thought for a few moments, then said, 'I'll do it.'

Charlton got to hear about the project which was being made by Paramount and, since he had just one last film to do for the studio, asked De Mille if he could play Jackson, thereby using up his contract at long last. Besides, he admired Jackson greatly and felt that a second stab at portraying him could prove most satisfying.

De Mille loved the idea of having Heston in his film and he directed his writers, Jesse Lasky Jr and Berenice Mosk, to expand the role of Jackson.

Heston eagerly set about the work of creating the make-up, basing Jackson's look on old paintings of him at the age of sixty. It was only when they were well into production that Heston suddenly realized that he'd made a dreadful mistake. Jackson, at the time the film was set, was only forty-six, yet Chuck was portraying him as an aged man.

Quinn had never directed before, but being an actor he was able to show the cast exactly how he expected them to play their parts by acting out all the roles himself for their benefit. However, not all the actors appreciated being told exactly how to perform. Heston, though, found Quinn to be a very gifted man who helped him add something to his performance with this technique. They worked so well together, in fact, that they discussed setting up further projects together, though nothing ever came to fruition.

De Mille was rarely on the set. When he was, he sat quietly to one side, although his shadow was very evident. But most of the time Quinn had the set and the cast and unit to himself. De Mille's active participation was limited to ordering a number of retakes (being unhappy with some of Quinn's work), and then to supervising the editing of the picture, which helped to add some of the old master's touch.

The Buccaneer is actually quite good; certainly not as bad as most critics have made out. Perhaps there is always some bias when an actor directs for the first time. In any event, Quinn has not directed since.

For his contribution to the film, De Mille gave Charlton that little wax statuette of Jackson which had sat in Heston's dressing-room during the filming of The President's Lady.

Even while The Buccaneer was in production, MGM were trying to seduce Heston into playing Messala in Ben-Hur op-

posite Burt Lancaster in the title role. Charlton felt most
uneasy about the prospect of playing the villain and Wyler,
now committed to the picture, did his best to reassure him. In
the meantime Lancaster pulled out of the film, somehow believing that the film would contradict his atheist views! A replacement was found – an Italian called Cesare Danova – but
Wyler had some misgivings about him, mainly because he
didn't have a particularly good command of the English
language. Wyler began wondering if Heston might not better
suit, and be suited to, the role of Ben-Hur.

Heston didn't hold his breath waiting for Wyler to make up
his mind. He was reunited with two of his fellow-performers
from *The Buccaneer*, Claire Bloom and E. G. Marshall, for a
TV production of *Beauty and the Beast* for CBS. It drew a huge
audience and received rave notices.

At last Wyler came to the decision that Heston should play
Ben-Hur, and Charlton eagerly grabbed the offer and
celebrated with Lydia and a bottle of champagne.

Before heading out for Italy, where *Ben-Hur* would be
made, Chuck did *Point of No Return* for Playhouse 90, directed
by Frank Schaffner. It was broadcast live on 20 February
1958.

Three weeks later, Charlton, Lydia and Fray were board-
ing the SS *United States* in New York, bound for Southampton and, ultimately, Rome and *Ben-Hur*.

# 12

# 'The Toughest Picture I Ever Made!'

IT WAS A LONG, LUXURIOUS CRUISE, MORE LIKE A MILLIONAIRE'S
vacation than a working voyage. The SS *United States* was littered with streamers and its passengers dizzy with vintage
champagne as the Hestons saw the Statue of Liberty for the

last time for another ten months.

The Atlantic crossing was leisurely and, had Charlton been able to foresee the toughest time of his life ahead of him, he would no doubt have drunk in every moment of freedom he was now allotted. But the holiday mood was over once they landed in Southampton. The Hestons boarded the train for London, and found themselves besieged by reporters, alerted by MGM who had, in fact, organized an arduous publicity build-up well before the cameras were to roll in Rome. Even when Charlton and his family arrived at the Dorchester Hotel – his favourite of all the London hotels – he was still fending off questions about a film he had not yet begun to make.

After further press calls in London, he was flown to Dublin to meet the press there, and then, *en route* to Rome, they stopped off in Paris to meet the French press. It was almost an entire month from their arrival in London before they actually arrived in Rome by train.

The Stazione Terminale was bubbling with movie fans and the Italian press. When the train pulled in and Charlton Heston emerged, a cry went up from the crowd, 'It is Moses! It is Moses!' A veritable mobbing ensued.

The Hestons were bundled into waiting Cadillacs and swept out of the station to the sumptuous villa where they would live in grandeur and luxury for the next ten months. They must have felt as though they had already set foot on the sets of *Ben-Hur*. The villa was stunningly classical with its marbled floors, arched frescoed ceilings and a series of fountains and classical statues.

The very next day – Lydia's birthday – they were at Alfredo's Restaurant where they had first come six years ago while on tour with the circus picture, and now he was to appear in a Roman circus!

There was a month to go before filming began, but still Charlton had his work cut out. His first task was to learn to drive a chariot under the guidance of famed stunt man and action director, Yakima Canutt. A year before Charlton set foot on the circus set, a thousand workmen had begun constructing the awesome arena, then the largest single set ever built for a motion picture. It had been carved out of a rock quarry at the far end of Cinecitta Studios, where the film was

to be shot, covering eighteen acres. Art director Edward Carfagno had modelled it after the ancient circus in Antioch,
where the race in the film is set.

The floor of the track, built on a rock foundation, was
covered with 40,000 tons of white sand transported from the
Mediterranean beaches. Behind the set stood wardrobe buildings, make-up tents, washrooms and a cafeteria equipped to
serve 5,000 people in twenty minutes.

A special practice track, the same size as the actual set, was
laid so that Heston, his co-star Stephen Boyd and seven
Hollywood stunt men could spend the next four to six weeks
training to be charioteers.

The race was like a complete motion picture in itself, with a
thirty-five-page script, completely separate from the full
screenplay, prepared by Yakima Canutt, outlining every
moment of action and all the stunt gags. Seventy horses from
Yugoslavia and eight from Sicily had been brought to Rome
for training under Glenn Randall six months prior to the start
of filming. By the time Charlton began working with them,
they knew a lot more about it than he did.

Canutt started Heston on a relatively docile team to train
with. He rode in the chariot with Charlton who manoeuvred
frantically with the reins, trying not to look terrified. Finally
Yak wordlessly stepped off the chariot while Heston, unaware he was now going solo, charged around the track.
Confident that his student charioteer could cope with the
ancient vehicle, Yak reported to William Wyler that Heston
would not have to be doubled for the filming. As Charlton
gained more confidence and his ability to handle a chariot grew,
Canutt moved him up on to tougher teams until, finally, all
the charioteers were ready to rehearse the race on the circus set.

'Listen, you guys,' Yak told the stunt men. 'Make it look
fast, dangerous and good, but let Chuck win, you hear!'

When Charlton expressed his concerns about racing with
all those seasoned stunt men, Yak assured him, 'Don't worry.
I guarantee you'll win the race.'

While Heston learned to be a charioteer, William Wyler
was frantically working on the script, trying to get it shootable – much of the dialogue was bland and some scenes were
still not in a final form. Karl Tunberg had written the original

screenplay, but with more work to do on it, Wyler, at the urging of Sam Zimbalist, brought Gore Vidal out to Rome to do the rewrites. But Wyler was dissatisfied and so playwright Christopher Fry found himself on the set in Rome and remained throughout filming. This was a crucial move, in Heston's estimate, and would lead to a small controversy involving him many months after filming was complete.

As far as what happened during the filming was concerned, he told me:

> I was very much aware of the two or three scenes on which Vidal submitted versions, and none of them seemed to me remarkable. And none was shot, despite whatever Gore Vidal might say.
>
> To the best of my memory, it was not Willy who suggested Christopher Fry. Sam Zimbalist, the producer, suggested it, and as soon as Fry came on Willy hit it off with him and obviously the material he submitted was very superior.
>
> In terms of total page count, a good percentage of it remained Karl Tunberg's who had done the version which Willy accepted when he undertook the assignment six or seven months earlier. But many crucial lines of dialogue were Fry's.

For the next few months, he split his time between shooting the race and working on the first unit with Wyler. His first real acting work on the picture was his opening sequence with Stephen Boyd as his boyhood friend, Messala. As they rehearsed over and over and shot take after take, Charlton began to feel that compared to this, shooting the chariot race was a picnic. Wyler had been tough on *The Big Country*, but now it seemed that nothing Charlton could do with his performance could please Wyler. He had never previously, and hasn't since, worked with such a demanding director.

He recalls:

> Working under him is certainly exhausting. He'll work doggedly at an idea from every conceivable angle until he's got what he wants, sometimes appearing to have no consideration for the people involved. Shooting a scene ten, fifteen, maybe twenty times is a common thing with

Willy, and he can be particularly telling on his actors in that his takes tend to be lengthy ones.

When Wyler still had not got what he wanted on the friendship scene, Chuck said to him, 'Willy, I just don't see what more we can get out of this. I'm really at a loss.'

Wyler replied, 'I know, but this is our only chance to show these two men as friends. If the audience can't believe that they love each other, then the fact that they come to hate each other is not going to interest them.'

In an effort to bring this scene to some satisfying conclusion, Charlton typed out a long memo to Wyler, outlining his ideas about the scene and the characters. It was a dreadful mistake. Wyler did not approve of his actors doing such things, and for the next couple of weeks Heston was in Wyler's bad books, and he was tougher than ever to please. At one time he even told Heston that he wasn't reaching anything like his full potential with the role. He was especially hard on Heston when Heston had little more to do in his scenes than listen and react to the other actors' lines.

Charlton had never felt himself under such pressure before, and he fought hard to please his director. He soon came to realize that Wyler purposely pressured him, virtually goading him into giving what would prove to be the performance of a lifetime. Wyler actually surprised Heston one time following the scene in the prison where Ben-Hur pleads with Messala to release his family. Such was his performance that the crew burst into spontaneous applause – and Wyler joined in with them. But Wyler never let up on his actors, particularly Heston who, after all, was carrying the weight of the film on his shoulders. If he failed in his part, the whole film would fail.

After one totally exhausting day, Wyler admitted to Charlton, 'I'd really like to be a nice guy on the set, but I can't make a good movie that way.' Heston realized, of course, that if anyone was under pressure, it was Wyler. Said Heston:

The pressure on him shooting *Ben-Hur* was so enormous. There was so much film that he printed and which the second unit printed on the chariot race, that for a time he fell very far behind and didn't get to look at it. Obviously he finally put in the time to run the 'dailies', and doing just that takes hours and hours. There's just no point in sitting there looking at them. You've got to be able to function creatively.

It was almost a relief to get back to the second unit to continue filming the chariot race. Wyler left all the master shots of the race to Canutt, involving himself only with the close-ups of Heston and Boyd, turning the race into not just a spectacle, but a personal conflict between two men. In fact, the majority of the race consists of these close-ups of two frantic and terrified actors.

The only notable shot of Ben-Hur in the race which Charlton did not do himself was the famous leap over the wrecked chariots. This was executed by Canutt's son, Joe. The gag had been meticulously planned and, like most stunts, you never knew if it would work until you tried it. A small hidden ramp was placed so that the chariot would leap up. Yak firmly instructed his son that when he did the leap, he was to hold the handrail, not at the front, but further back with his hands far apart, or he would chance being flipped out over the top to probable death.

Joe jumped into the chariot and raced down the track while Yakima sat behind the camera. As his son approached the wreckage, Yak's heart almost stopped. He saw that Joe's hands were close together at the front of the handrail. The horses jumped over, the chariot hit the ramp and flew up. Joe shot up in the air, tossed like a pancake, and came crashing to the ground. Miraculously, he survived.

Distressed at his son's near-fatal accident, but elated by what he had captured on film, Canutt shot some close-ups of Heston climbing back into the chariot and edited it into the footage of Joe so that it looked as though Ben-Hur had been flipped out but had not fallen, managing to scramble back into the still charging chariot and win the race.

With the race finally over, Heston began work on a totally new part of the film, including a new second unit, this time headed by Andrew Marton whose job was to shoot the galley slave sequences and the sea battle.

Heston's first scene in this portion of the production was

set in the Roman villa of Quintus Arrius, played by Jack
Hawkins. The villa was an exquisite creation, highlighted by
five fountains fed by almost nine miles of water pipes. He
found it easy working with Hawkins who, in the scene,
adopts Ben-Hur as his son. There was much in Charlton's
own past life, as well as in Hawkins's sensitive delivery, that
made his reactions to Arrius' speech real and convincing.

Filming the galley slaves sequences was the toughest thing
Charlton had yet done. The set was claustrophobic and
unbearably hot. His back hurt when he and the other extras
portraying the slaves had to undergo a strenuous series of
speed changes.

For the exterior scenes of the galley, a man-made lake was
dug and two full-sized galleys placed on it. The long shots of
the battle were also filmed in the lake, using effective minia-
ture galleys.

Towards the end of filming, in the autumn of 1958, Sam
Zimbalist dropped dead of a heart attack. William Wyler
took complete charge of the production and was paid hand-
somely for it. But he was worth every penny. Not long after
Zimbalist's death, news came through that Tyrone Power
had died on the set of *Solomon and Sheba* in Spain. Charlton
was pulled up sharply and began to consider his own physical
condition. The fact was, he was running down.

He said:

I guess *Ben-Hur* was the toughest picture I ever made,
simply because it went on the longest. You find you begin
to use yourself up. We shot for nine months, and it wasn't
like the Burton-Taylor *Cleopatra* where they sat around.
We shot *every* day, ten or twelve hours a day, six days a
week – sometimes seven– and I worked first and second
unit. If I wasn't working for Wyler on the first unit, I was
riding a chariot or rowing a galley. So I'm not kidding
when I say I worked every day, *all* day. And towards the
end of it, say about the seventh month, I was honestly getting into a thing where I'd be driven to work in a limo and
I'd be lying in the back and thinking, 'Let's see; if I got
killed or broke my leg, could they finish the picture? I
wonder how they could shoot around me. They could use a

double, sort of over the shoulder. And they don't really need that other scene.' And finally I'm sorting out the scenes they absolutely had to have, and I'm thinking, 'God, *please* let them finish the picture.'

I guess that was the only picture I've ever done at the end of which I felt not only my total physical energies but also my total creative energies beginning to frazzle out.

I would say – and I've heard Olivier say this, and always feel perfectly confident about repeating anything on which Laurence Olivier agrees – a very important ingredient for a successful actor, certainly a successful director, is physical energy and good health because you not only need to be there but you need to be at your best. If you're not right up at your peak, you're not going to do good work, so you have to be able to sleep at night – I can sleep anywhere; in limos or make-up chairs or backs of station wagons or sound chapman booms [microphones] or cliffs – and not run down, and be there and healthy. That may not sound glamorous or inspirational, but believe me, it counts.

Finally, in January 1959, he wound up on the film. At the time he said:

Nine months is an exceptional time to be on one film. I'll confess I'm glad it's over. Like mountaineering, it's tough while you're at it, but leaves you with a sense of achievement. I shan't feel satisfied though until I've seen the final film.

When he did see the finished film, he was delighted, feeling that it was, after all, worth all the blood and sweat he'd spilled into the Italian sand. There followed a series of fabulous, glittering *premières*, including a Royal Première at the Empire Theatre in London's Leicester Square. The American critics certainly liked the picture, but the London newspapers were positively overwhelmed by it.

Some of them ran thus:

This is the ultimate Epic... Think of everything you expect from a film and *Ben-Hur* has it. It also has something

you have never seen before. The chariot race is the most
exciting thing since moving pictures were invented...
Only one thing worries me: How on earth can anybody
outdo *Ben-Hur*? (*Daily Herald*)

Fabulous!... You will be moved to tears. Your nerves
will be strung to screaming point. You will marvel. A
mighty picture which massively, courageously, tastefully
and honourably brings a story of Christ to the screen...
You are not watching a film. You are experiencing it – the
ultimate achievement in the art of movie-making. (*Daily
Mirror*)

*Ben-Hur* leaves everything standing. Can the movies ever
excel this terrific excitement? I don't think so. (*Evening
News*)

Other reviews were shot through with such acclaims as, 'A
wonderful story, magnificently told' (*Daily Telegraph*); 'Will
be memorable in the history of the cinema' (*The Times*); 'A
celluloid phenomenon' (*Daily Express*); 'Never have the most
moving moments in man's history been more movingly told'
(*The Star*); 'The story has an inspired excitement, mystery
magic' (*People*).
   Perhaps the *News of the World* best summed it up when it
said, '*Masterpiece* – that's *Ben-Hur*. You *must* see it.'

Charlton was in New York, stumbling under the weight of
*The Tumbler*, and delighting in the direction of Laurence Olivier, but suffering from a critical and commercial response to
the play, when Bill Blowitz called.
   'Chuck, I've just heard – you've been nominated for an
Oscar for *Ben-Hur*.'
   'Well, Bill,' said Charlton, 'that's damned nice.'
   And it was even more so on the big night when Susan Hayward read out his name as Best Actor of the year. Heston
kissed Lydia and made his way to the stage, fighting back a
sudden attack of stage fright. He arrived, dripping with perspiration, to collect his statuette, and thanked William Wyler,

MGM, Yakima Canutt, the members of the Academy, and Christopher Fry. He didn't know it then, but the very mention of Fry at the Academy Awards had the chairman and the board of the Writers' Guild reaching for their typewriters to protest aganst Heston's audacity.

What had happened was, the Writers' Guild, of which Christopher Fry was not a member, refused to allow Fry screen credit for *Ben-Hur*, and so only Karl Tunberg's name went up. The screenplay had received a nomination, but the Academy, recognizing the Guild's refusal to give Fry any credit, did not vote for the *Ben-Hur* screenplay. The film did, however, go on to win Oscars for Best Director and Best Film, claiming a total eleven Oscars, more than any film before or since has won.

The newspapers made quite a meal of the protesting letter Heston received from the Guild, publishing it as well as Heston's reply to them. Heston was, in fact, unmoved and rightly unrepentant. He said to me:

In my judgement, and in Wyler's, it was a gross injustice to deny Fry credit, and is obviously the reason that *Ben-Hur* didn't sweep all the twelve awards for which it was nominated. The only one it didn't win was best screenplay because it was generally known within the Academy that Fry had not received any credit, and they therefore didn't want to vote the writing award to Karl Tunberg.

But the important thing for Charlton was that he had come away clutching an Oscar, an award which, in more recent times, it has become popular to belittle in some quarters. But to Heston it was a moment of recognition which he sought and desired. When I asked him just what the Oscar meant to him, he said:

A great deal! A *great* deal! Obviously, for one thing, it's going to mean a lot of money to you. But I think the reason that the Academy Award is pre-eminent among film makers is that it represents the opinion of your peers.

The other awards are given by juries or critics and

they're very nice to have. But the opinion of people who do the same work you do is what you most want, and that's what the Academy Award is.

And that's what Charlton Heston had.

# Part Three

## 13

# He Goes Forth Gallantly

HE WATCHED AS THE DOUBLE-DECKERED CINE BUSES RUMBLED into Almeria at long last, like long-awaited reinforcements. He felt a little like a General directing his tank command, and became even more frustrated when it became clear that the buses would not be able to get close enough to the Alcazaba Castle because of low overhead wires. But at least they were there, so that Charlton would be able to hold his editing conferences and view the dailies of *Antony and Cleopatra* while still out among the sand dunes of the small but nevertheless sun-beaten desert of Almeria.

At last it was all coming together. Ever since he had played on Broadway in *Antony and Cleopatra*, that play had run through his mental moviola a million times. Since he won his Oscar for *Ben-Hur* eleven years ago, he had fulfilled that prophecy the *Dark City* posters had foreseen; he had become a force on the screen, and never more so than now, in 1971, as he helmed the most creative, most exciting project of his career – the making of Shakespeare's *Antony and Cleopatra* into a motion picture. He had his own money riding on this. It was a risk he had to take – a risk he wanted to take.

He had been involved with the setting up of films before, although his role as an actor had always been predominant then. But now, as co-producer with Peter Snell, he was feeling the full weight of the enormous responsibilities that a motion picture brings. Since his arrival in Spain, ahead of all his actors, he had faced, and solved, one challenge after another. The roof on the largest sound stage in Spain, at Sevilla Studios, had fallen in, leaving them with no stage large enough in the country on which to shoot the palace interiors. Compromises had to be made; extra costs incurred. And then the cine buses had been held up in Bilbao by customs and released only after Heston had paid a bond. They arrived just the day before shooting was due to commence.

Now they couldn't get the buses into the Alcazaba, the castle where the Roman-style roof and the white buildings perfectly doubled for Rome and Egypt and where Charlton had discovered a perfect gladiatorial arena. But he just knew that by tomorrow everything would be in order and ready to go. He checked over his sets in the castle one more time. There stood portions of Caesar's palace and, at the back, a gate for the farewell scene between Antony and Caesar. He checked on his cast. All but Carmen Sevilla, who was to play Octavia, were there – Sevilla wouldn't be there for another four days. There had been so much to schedule, so much to reschedule.

Not long ago he had spent an evening with director and friend Frank Schaffner. Over a glass of whisky, Charlton had said, 'Frank, I think I'm going to direct this picture.'

'Why not?' said Frank. 'Nothing to it.'

Now it was all about to happen, and Charlton Heston was about to direct his first major motion picture. He has since said that directing a picture is much like conducting a military operation. If so, he was ready for the great battle.

*He goes forth gallantly: that he and Caesar might*
*Determine this great war in single fight!*
*Then Antony – but now –.*

# 14

# Return to Actor's Country

CHARLTON HAD NEVER RECEIVED SUCH A RADICAL OFFER: TO
*direct* a film on the life of Christ! *Ben-Hur* had only just been
premiered, *The Ten Commandments* was still doing the
rounds, and Charlton Heston was already considered something of an authority on biblical pictures. It wasn't at all surprising that he was suddenly being sent every epic script in
town, but to *direct* one?

That chariot race had certainly sent the dust flying. His
status in the industry was, in 1960, such that he was considered both as important and authoritative as any actor in
Hollywood. And actors were suddenly in vogue as directors also.
John Wayne was behind and in front of the cameras on *The
Alamo*, Marlon Brando was having delusions of adequacy
directing *One-Eyed Jacks*, and Laurence Olivier had proven
that he was the best Shakespearean movie director in the world.

So Heston shouldn't have been too surprised when, just
two months after being offered the film on Christ to direct,
that MCA should come through with another offer to direct a
picture, promising him two million dollars!

But, as with the previous offer, he turned it down. He just
didn't feel he could direct pictures. And he simply didn't
want to direct; a view he would maintain over the years until
the time came when he felt he could not afford to see the project of a lifetime slip away from him.

As an actor, he was now in a stronger position than ever
before. Wanting to do something more modest with which to
follow *Ben-Hur*, Heston chose to do *The Wreck of the Mary
Deare* with Gary Cooper. The film really belonged to Cooper
with Heston playing a secondary role. It was Cooper's penul-
timate picture, before dying of cancer. But during the
making of it, he and Heston struck up a warm friendship that
endured until Cooper's death.

The film's most exciting sequence was its opening one in which Heston, as a salvager, comes across a drifting ship, the *Mary Deare*, on fire and mysteriously abandoned in a storm. Securing a rope to the ship, Heston climbs aboard.

This scene was shot in the MGM water tank set, and director Michael Anderson considered using a stunt man to double for Heston scrambling up the side of a rolling ship while fake waves rocked the salvager's smaller boat against the ship's hull and wind machines lashed every part of the set with stinging water spray.

Anderson told me:

It was very dangerous. I offered Chuck a double, but he sized it up and assessed it and felt that I could come in close with the camera, and if I wanted to be close enough to see who it was, then he'd rather do it himself. So he did it all himself, and you could see it was him, so it was worth it.

But it wasn't quite as simple as Chuck had expected it to be. He'd practised rope climbing in the studio gym, but it was a whole new experience with all that wind and spray and rolling sets. Hauling himself up, he suddenly felt a searing pain in his leg, weakening him considerably. All the while the cameras were turning, and he knew he couldn't give up on the scene. There were just ten feet to go, and he continued to haul himself up, clambering over the rail and allowing himself to roll on to the deck, groaning with the pain. Unaware that he had been hurt, Anderson called out, 'Let's do it one more time, Chuck.'

'Sorry Mike,' replied Heston, 'but you'd better print that one.'

Only then did the director realize that Charlton had been hurt. He was carted off to the studio surgery and given heat treatment for a suspected torn ligament. As the pain subsided he returned to work that day, and indeed, he didn't miss a single day's filming, but even though the ligament proved to be undamaged, he was unable to repeat the rope climb. Nevertheless, the footage that Anderson had captured was more than sufficient, setting the tone for the film as Heston discovers the captain, Gary Cooper, driving the ship on to a reef to sink it, thereby igniting the mystery with which to occupy the rest of the film's running time.

Mid-way during shooting, Heston was given time off so that he could do *Macbeth* at Ann Arbor, Michigan. In fact, MGM rescheduled their film just so Charlton could do that 'man-killer' part again.

Although John O'Shaughnessy directed, Heston himself adapted and cut the play. It felt good to be back in actor's country, although the play was put together so fast and the run was so short that he was still hungry for it when it closed. He'd certainly left his mark on the play. Because of the control he exercised over the cutting, he had, as before, and since, included the horrific beheading sequence which was so often left out of other productions because of its gory nature. Heston points out that the beheading is 'one of the few stage directions in Shakespeare that are authentically Shakespearean.' He also maintains that 'it's the tragic catharsis at the end of four acts of the greatest drama there is.'

Although by no means the only American actor to do Shakespeare, it is his sharp understanding of the work that has made him one of the very few and probably most notable of American actors to play Shakespeare successfully.

He returned to Hollywood to continue with *Mary Deare* and even spent a little time in England shooting scenes at Elstree Studios. The work itself wasn't particularly stimulating, especially after *Macbeth*, but he revelled in the companionship of Gary Cooper, and they often dined together.

*The Wreck of the Mary Deare* was hardly the most satisfying film to make, and Charlton was in no real hurry to get to work on another film. He was homesick for actor's country, particularly with the short and tantalizing run of *Macbeth* making him thirsty for more stage work. Film scripts were pouring in, but Chuck chose to do *State of the Union* in Santa Barbara, California – and Lydia was going to be in it with him. They'd last done that play back in North Carolina at the Thomas Wolfe Memorial Theater, so it was a property they both knew.

They had just one week to put the show together. The first few days were chaotic and the cast were hardly experienced enough to work at the pace the schedule demanded. Heston was frustrated with the progress and took an active hand in getting the play into some semblance of order. When it opened it was a disaster. By the time it closed after the scheduled five days, it was an improvement on the first performance, but it was not a theatrical experience to remember. Charlton could not foresee the greater and more painful disaster to come – *The Tumbler*.

The house at Coldwater Canyon was finally built. According to Charlton's specifications, it seemed to be made of little more than glass. Its most prominent feature was a terrace outside the second-floor bedroom, jutting out over the canyon. The drop below was dizzying; a strange bit of architecture considering Heston feared heights. Yet here he felt secluded from the hustle of Los Angeles below; it seemed positively inpregnable. Jolly West, Heston's good friend, once told him, 'You know Chuck, this is ideal for pouring burning oil on invaders.'

'You bet,' said Heston. 'Up here, they can't get me.'

Unfortunately, the house was not immune from the sometimes extreme hazards that California's elements caused. Even before they moved in, the house was damaged by a bush fire that had swept through Bel Air, though fortunately the damage was superficial compared to the fate of other buildings in the neighbourhood. Since then the house has managed to withstand just about everything Nature has hurled at it, and it has come to be known as 'the house that *Ben-Hur* built,' because the Hestons finally paid for it with the money Charlton earned from that picture, which was considerable to say the least.

The house was still slightly damaged by the fire when they moved in – rather hurriedly since Charlton was due to fly off to New York to do another play, *The Tumbler*. It was to be directed by Laurence Olivier. If ever Heston had a hero, it was Olivier. He has often said that there has never been a greater actor than Laurence Olivier, and when it came to a decision as to whether he should do the play with Olivier or go with an offer from Twentieth Century-Fox to do a Marilyn Monroe film, Olivier won hands down.

*The Tumbler* was written by Benn Levy in blank verse, and told the bizarre story of a farmer, played by Heston, who becomes obsessed by a beautiful young girl who later discovers that he is in fact her stepfather and suspects that he had murdered her real father. She eventually drives him to hang himself. Rosemary Harris was cast as the girl, and as the farmer's haggard old wife was Hermione Baddeley.

Rehearsals in New York began excitingly enough, with Olivier assembling his cast in his hotel suite and acting out all the parts himself. As rehearsals progressed, Heston began to realize that it was not going to be an easy play to bring off. His greatest motivation was in being directed by Olivier. Working with him on a play was as exciting as being directed by Orson Welles in a film. For the first time in his career, though, Charlton began to feel daunted by the role. He felt barely adequate, could not achieve any level of conviction and he positively sought for Olivier to get at him and bring out the performance that just had to be inside of him somewhere.

They opened the play in Boston where the flaws in the performances and in the writing became painfully obvious. A whole new opening sequence was written and Olivier began cutting the play, to Benn Levy's distress. They had no other recourse than to tighten it and chop out much of the dialogue. Also, it became apparent that Hermione Baddeley was inadequate and so Martha Scott replaced her as the wife, much to Charlton's delight. On two previous occasions, in *Ben-Hur* and *The Ten Commandments*, Scott had played Heston's mother. Now she was his wife! The play improved with the recasting and the re-editing, but throughout the run, Olivier dropped in new pieces, took out old ones, reintroduced scenes and dialogue previously dropped, desperately fashioning it for the Broadway run.

As exciting as it was to work with Olivier, it was a profoundly difficult and sometimes totally unhappy project to be involved in. Olivier was suffering personal problems as his marriage to Vivien Leigh fell apart. But he continued to pour his energies into the play and enjoyed working with Heston so much that he hoped to find more projects for them to collaborate on. He went so far as to tell Heston, 'You can be the greatest actor in America in my lifetime.'

But not even the heroic efforts by everyone concerned could save the play. The day after it opened on Broadway the newspaper reviews sent the entire cast into a depression. All but two were scathing. Of the good ones, *The New York Times* described Heston's performance as 'massive, masculine and fluent', while *The New Yorker* said that Heston was 'wry, verbose, and sexy ... speaking lines with a leaden thrust.' Such personal notices were not enough to appease Heston who felt as if he never did manage one single performance more than adequately. At times he could be quite magnificent in the first half and poor in the next. Then he'd fall flat for the first half of the next performance and rise to the occasion for the final scenes.

The other reviews were literally killers. They murdered the play, and that night the closing notice went up. They did just one more night and in so doing gave the best run-through of all. Says Heston of *The Tumbler*:

> I'm the only one who came out of it with any profit. The producers lost money, and Benn Levy lost months' worth of work because of it. Larry Olivier lost out too. But I got out of it precisely what I went in for – the chance to work with Olivier. I learned more from him in six weeks than I ever would have learned otherwise. I think I ended up a better actor, with more responsibility.

# 15

# *Campeador*

RONALD REAGAN MAY HAVE BEEN LITTLE MORE THAN A GRADE-B picture star, but he had a commanding presence. And maybe as an actor his talent was limited, but as a politician his gift is unmeasurable. It's not surprising, therefore, that between the years 1947 and 1952 Reagan served as president of the Screen Actors Guild.

CAMPEADOR 103

In 1959 he was reinstated as president of the SAG at a time when the actors' union was battling to earn for its membership a share of the profits that the studios were making from their sales of movies to television. Ironically, the cinema was suffering because of the expanding television market, but the studios had found that there was still gold in their old products which the TV networks were anxious to buy and pay well for. But the stars of these pre-1948 movies didn't get so much as a dime from TV sales. The Guild wanted to take action.

They chose Reagan as the man best suited to 'excite the membership, stir them up', as one Guild member put it. About 14,000 actors looked to Reagan to come up with the goods that would give them a share of the profits from TV sales. He took the case to the studios, demanding they make provision to share their profits with the performers. But the studios turned the Guild down flat.

On 7 March 1960, Reagan called the first strike ever in the history of the SAG which had been in existence since 1933. There was a sudden silence that fell over the sets and sound stages of movie studios all over Hollywood. No actor reported for work and every movie in production was forced to shut down.

It was a time of crisis in the film industry, and Charlton Heston, as much as any other SAG member, felt the tension and unease that settled upon the acting community of Los Angeles. But instead of sitting around brooding and waiting for the crisis to pass, he decided to find another play rather than wait for motion picture production to start again.

Meanwhile, Reagan was reshaping the directorship of the Guild, building strength with which to combat the stubborn studios who seemed unable to accept that the days of the old studio system where they controlled everything were over. An invitation came to Heston for him to join the board of directors. He felt a political stirring from within, and accepted. Just about his very first job as a member of the board was to join the special negotiating committee, headed by Reagan, which met with the studio heads. The strike had so far run a full month, and both actors and studios were desperate to bring it to an end.

They sat around tables for a whole day, discussing, arguing, accusing, shouting, calming down and, eventually, agreeing on terms. Heston emerged tired like the rest, but exhilarated by the experience. There was a sense of pride which he felt at having been part of an historic moment in the history of Hollywood. It was also, though neither he nor anyone else may have seen it then, a decisive move for the years to come when almost brand-new films were to fill much of the time on both network television and cable TV.

As for Heston, films such as *Ben-Hur* and other hugely successful films still to be made, would sell to television for vast amounts of money, ensuring that he at least would benefit from the very agreement he had helped to formulate even in decades to come. Whether he could have realized that or not, his sudden political involvement as a director of the SAG board added to his stature, and he was never again quite the same kind of actor. Neither was he quite the same kind of citizen. The simple backwoods hick from Michigan was evolving into a political animal, and before long would become one of the most influential and authoritative actors in the business.

The strike had considerably slowed down the turnout of scripts, and the paucity of really good movie projects offered to him was not something he panicked over. He could afford to be discriminating in his search for quality and commercial success. But as he read one lousy script after another, his spirits sank.

There was, however, one idea that intrigued him. It was the story of El Cid, the semi-legendary knight of eleventh-century Spain. Philip Yordan, who had written *The Naked Jungle*, was fashioning the screenplay, and producer Samuel Bronston promised Heston he'd be the first to see the finished screenplay.

When it finally reached him he could hardly believe how bad it was. It was midsummer and the sun beat down on Coldwater Canyon. Charlton was decidedly uncomfortable in the sweltering heat, and he was in no mood for such appalling material. He rang Herman Citron and told him to tell Bronston he wasn't interested.

But Bronston, and his director Anthony Mann, wanted nobody else but Heston to play the Cid. They believed only the man who could personify Moses and Ben-Hur could hope to bring the Cid, a semi-legendary character, to real life. They continued to push, and Charlton reluctantly agreed to reconsider if they could rewrite the script to his satisfaction. They grabbed at the chance and Yordan went to work on the rewrite.

Charlton immediately immersed himself in research on the Cid and was frustrated to find very little. In fact, the legend of El Cid has very much overshadowed history because just about all there is written on the man is the *poema del mio Cid*. It was the legend that the film was more concerned with.

El Cid was in reality Rodrigo Diaz de Bivar who won his name – (a Spanish form of the Arabic 'sayyid' 'the Lord') – from his enemies, the Moors who threatened Christian Spain. He was later exiled by his King, Alfonso, yet he remained loyal to him and won for him the crown of Valencia even though he had the power and the support from his followers to take the crown himself. Loved passionately by his wife, and fervently supported by his followers, the Cid rode into legend when, having died in battle, he was strapped to his horse to lead his troops to the final, ultimate victory over the Moors.

That was the legend that the film wanted to capture, and most of it was accurate. However, in reality Rodrigo was not the saint that the *poema* makes him out to be, although he did remain unbelievably loyal to Alfonso. It also seems that he married twice, although both women shared the same name, Jimena or Ximena. The screenplay blended them into one woman, Chimene. History also shows that the Cid never led his men into battle while strapped dead to his horse. But then the picture was never intended to be anything more than a semi-historical, semi-legendary portrayal of the Cid, and it was this concept that seemed to captivate Charlton.

'El Cid was surely one of the remarkable men of the Middle Ages,' he says. 'And he – as is true with almost any such figure from that period where literal documentation is so

sparse – has become a mythical figure of legendary propor-
tions.'

The film was certainly a mammoth project, and had to be
assembled bit by bit. Heston had been the first piece of this
complicated jigsaw around which to build the rest of the picture. Bronston and Mann had secured him before the script
was completed, and even when it was finished it was still far
from perfect. Only after Heston arrived in Madrid to begin
work on the film was Sophia Loren cast as Chimene. She,
however, was available for a mere ten weeks, while Heston
was going to be there for six months at least, so the shooting
schedule became complex in that all of Loren's shots had to be
done first, even though she would be seen in scenes running
throughout the finished picture.

There were further complications when Loren brought her
own writer to translate her dialogue into Italian, and then
back into English with her changes. This time-consuming
technique tested Heston's patience until he got so mad over
the hold-ups that he had crossed words with Mann who, after
all, was supposed to be in control.

It became an increasingly more difficult film to make.
While Charlton liked to get on with the work, he didn't care
to be pushed, and everyone was pushed for time to get all of
Sophia's scenes on film before her ten weeks were up.
Towards the end of her allotted time, Charlton's professional
tolerance was severely strained when she began arriving late
on the set. In fact, when she turned up predictably late for the
scene where the Cid dies, he was so furious that he refused to
even speak or look at her. He's a little more amused by the
episode now. As he told me with good humour:

Like Spencer Tracy once said, I come to work on time, I
know my lines and I don't bump into the furniture. It's
probably something of a neurosis with me. I don't like
people who come late and, I must admit, my reaction is
excessive.

But my neurosis is cheaper than theirs!

However, I think I've become a little more tolerant than
when I worked with Sophia. A great many women come
late to the set. It's more difficult for actresses than for

actors. The physical pressures are much greater. The anxieties more pressing. It often manifests itself in terms of an excessive preoccupation with how they look, which is understandable. I was just less tolerant of it then.

With Sophia finished up and homeward bound, some of the more physical scenes began to take precedence, and there was certainly plenty of physical stuff for Heston to do. Probably more than in any other film up until that time.

For two hours every morning Italian fencing master Enzo Musemici Greco put Heston through gruelling practice sessions with swords, maces and lances, putting him in 'the best shape of my entire career'. Heston is a man who learns physical skills with amazing aptitude. Said Anthony Mann, 'Charlton is the ideal actor for the epic. Apart from his physical attributes, he can handle a horse, a sword, a chariot, a lance, anything, as though he were made for it. He's incredible. Put a toga on him and he looks perfect.' Says Charlton:

I have to be fit. If I wasn't, these parts would almost kill me. I make a point of doing regular work-outs in every spare minute I can get.

I find tennis is the ideal game to play. It's wonderful exercise, particularly when playing in the hot sun. But, you know, I put on weight so easily. So I spend most of my time trying to lose it. I'm a critical observer of my waistline.

As well as playing tennis at every opportunity, he also walked each and every day, increasing the mileage until he was pacing five miles a day. Not surprisingly, he lost twelve pounds before the end of filming.

As shooting progressed, Charlton came to care very much for the picture, believing it could be the greatest epic film of all time. But he also felt that Anthony Mann just wasn't the right man to direct El Cid. He was critical of the way Mann insisted on directing the big battle scenes himself, utilizing the 6,000 extras portraying Spanish and Moorish warriors, instead of leaving the action to second unit director Yakima Canutt.

Heston voiced his disapproval, and eventually persuaded Bronston and Mann to give Canutt one day on his own to work on some of the battle cuts. But, in Heston's estimation, even the added footage couldn't give the *El Cid* battles the sweep and drama that they cried out for. He told me:

It was a great, great error on Tony's part. Many directors, particularly nowadays, feel threatened by a second unit director. They feel their creative authority or their final reputation will in some way be blemished by surrendering to a second unit director the control of that scene. I think this is a great mistake.

Wyler felt secure enough to turn over the chariot race. George Stevens did the same thing. To the best of my knowledge, John Huston does. There are scenes like that where a second unit director is simply able to do it better and leaves the director free for really more important work.

This doesn't mean that the first unit director doesn't consult with him and say, 'Now I want you to be sure to get this shot and that shot.' Of course he does. But in the first place those sequences are enormously time-consuming to shoot and the first unit director would take even longer to shoot them. That's what Tony's problem was. It took him even longer to do it, and he didn't do it as well as Canutt could. And the things he can do well are meanwhile not being done.

Tony Mann, rest his soul, was a decent man and a good film-maker. But he made terrible mistakes and missed his chance of having *El Cid* be the greatest epic film ever made, because it's by far and away the best story of any epic film.

Physically, in visual terms, it's a beautiful film, and I bitterly regret that it fell so short of its potential. The potential, of course lies in the dimensions of the character. But any great film is largely the work of the director. Therefore, it's fair to lay at least some of the blame on the director.

One of the problems with the film, as with any epic film, is that they tend to be rather thin on the ground with their character development. They have so many characters to introduce, such a complexity of historical events to get through, that you tend to skim over or eliminate entirely the kind of scene that fills out a character. This is certainly true of *El Cid*.

If only Tony Mann had concentrated his creative energies on directing the actors and left all the action to Yak Canutt, *El Cid* could well have been the greatest epic film ever.

I think it's a very fine film. But not great.

Actually, *El Cid* is generally regarded by critics and audiences alike as being one of the superior screen epics of the late Fifties and early Sixties. It's also fair to say that, despite Heston's criticisms, Anthony Mann, who died seven years later, captured some wonderful images, particularly of the dead Cid astride his white horse riding like a spectre into the enemy. This final sequence brought the film to its legendary pinnacle, and Mann succeeded in bringing the myth to life, making it an historic film that remains firmly rooted in legend.

Filming this last scene actually proved pretty tricky for Heston who had to look completely lifeless without falling off his horse. He told me:

They strapped a brace across the shoulders which came up from the saddle. Beyond that, I simply had to hold myself stiff with my hand wired to the lance.

But it was a curious thing because it's remarkably hard to ride that way. It isn't a question of controlling him. He'll go. If you kick a horse, he'll more or less go in a straight line, especially if you've ridden him once or twice before. Horses are creatures of habit and they'll go where you've ridden them. Now, I'm a fair horseman, but you don't realize until you try to sit a horse without moving just how many saddle weight adjustments go on all the time when you're riding. If you try to sit absolutely motionless, you feel the whole thing gradually shifting to one side or the other, and finally you have to cheat a little bit and put some weight on one stirrup or the other, or you fall off.

The very last sequence filmed was the trial by combat by which the Cid won another title, 'Campeador' ('Champion') from his king. Filmed next to the beautifully preserved castle of Belmonte, the sequence took some four weeks of preparation and filming. This time Yakima Canutt told Anthony Mann to leave the second unit to him or he'd have to find another stunt director. Mann stepped down and filmed only the dialogue and the build-up to the fight.

Joe Canutt again doubled Heston as he had done for the chariot race. Joe's contribution was mainly being toppled from his horse and, later, bringing his opponent's horse down in a dangerous manoeuvre. Other than those shots, Charlton did just about everything himself.

Despite his own reservations about the film, it received healthy reviews and quickly became a box-office champion. Released in 1961, it grossed in its first year more than $35 million, and a year later it was approaching $50 million. For a time it was ahead of *Ben-Hur* which earlier had become the second-highest grossing film of all time – *Gone with the Wind* being first. In fact, prior to *Ben-Hur*, *The Ten Commandments* was the second-highest grossing film ever, and before that it was *The Greatest Show on Earth*. Charlton Heston's films were making more money than any other star's at that time.

After ten years in pictures, Charlton Heston was the cinema's own 'Campeador'.

# 16

# A Bad Case of Misjudgement

HE STOOD WITH THE OTHER PICKETS, WEARING A SANDWICH-board that let the citizens of Oklahoma City know that he for one deplored the segregation of blacks from whites in that

city's restaurants. It had been a sudden decision, following
the suggestion by his friend Jolly West that he join in the pick-
eting of the city's restaurants. It was, after all, supposed to be
a vacation along with a dozen other of his friends and family.
They'd set out about a week earlier, congregating in St
Helen, then heading up to Two Rivers and continuing west in
a convoy of cars and trucks.

The very idea of the man who played Moses striking a note
in favour of the negroes was enough to bring the reporters
flocking to the scene. It was a very peaceful affair. Perhaps the
racists were unnerved at having Moses there to tell them to
repent. But the black folk were eager to voice their thanks,
and Charlton Heston, just by wearing a sandwich-board, had
become something of a real-life hero.

The story was put out over the wires all over the country,
and Heston's name was prominent. It all began to look a little
too much like a publicity stunt, which dismayed Heston, and
before he knew it he was conducting interviews on the
matter, such was the demand by the press to make a meal of
the incident. It was a relief when they were able to get going
again on their journey, and as they crossed the state line into
California, they all burst into song: 'California, here I
come . . . !'

He was back home for the first time since he'd left to do *El
Cid*. But he wasn't home for long. Two weeks later he was on
his way to Berlin at the request of the State Department to
attend the Berlin Festival as their official delegate. He was
beginning to feel that the home he had long dreamed of was
becoming little more than a place to holiday in between his
trans-Atlantic jaunts which were becoming increasingly
more frequent.

It was a momentous time to be in Berlin. It was also
depressing. The tension between East and West was intensi-
fied in the German capital. Touring the Eastern sector, he was
not impressed with what he saw of Communist life. He was
unrestricted in his movement, carrying a diplomatic passport, but he was relieved to return to the Western sector
again. A few days later, the Berlin Wall was sealed up and the
gulf between East and West widened.

Finally leaving Berlin behind, Charlton and Lydia flew

straight to Chicago to the house where his mother, Lilla, still lived and where the young misfit from St Helen first began to spread his acting wings.

There were four of them now – Charlton, Lydia, Fray and now baby Holly. Since the birth of Fray, six years previously, Lydia had not managed to conceive, and so they decided to adopt. Prior to *El Cid* Charlton and Lydia had undergone a series of interviews with the adoption board. In the summer of 1961 they were finally able to bring their new daughter home. She had been born on 1 August. She was just sixteen days old.

With the family complete, Charlton became aware, more than ever before, of the family instinct within him. Much of it was to do with the bitter memories of those traumatic days when Russ and Lilla divorced and little Charlton had been carted off to the city to experience fear of both his new environment and the future without dad. But perhaps, most of all, it was to do with the security he felt within the walls of his own home with a family of his own and the financial security which was theirs.

But still there was little time to enjoy it. Before long he was back in Europe again, to film *The Pigeon that Took Rome*. It was a war-time comedy directed, produced and written by Melville Shavelson for Paramount. They originally intended to make the whole picture in Italy, but when they learned of Heston's reluctance to spend more time away from home than was necessary, they rescheduled, shooting first on location and then returning to Hollywood for the interiors.

By now Charlton seemed to be naturally suspicious of his leading ladies, and when he met Elsa Martinelli, an Italian beauty who was co-starring with him in the picture, he was immediately aware of what he foresaw as difficulties regarding her English. But what really raised his hackles was when she began arriving late. Eventually, frustrated with the difficulty he felt she was having with her dialogue, he took an active hand in getting her through her performance, the first time he had ever interfered with another actor's work.

He finished the film in time for them to spend their first

Christmas at Coldwater, and an old tradition was perpetu-
ated from years ago by having a tree felled on Charlton's own
land in Michigan and erected in their home.

The New Year saw numerous irons in the fire. He signed
to do *55 Days at Peking*, again for Samuel Bronston, and *Diamond Head*, a contemporary film set in Hawaii. He also
bought the rights to a play he had once been offered but was
unable to do called *The Lovers*. It was the story of a Norman
knight who takes another man's bride for his lover. Heston
felt that it would make a fine film, and so he purchased the
screen rights, determining that it would be a small-budget,
intimate film. With the support of Walter Seltzer, now producing pictures instead of publicizing them, he went ahead in
his search for someone to fashion Leslie Stevens's play into a
superior screenplay. The man they came up with was John
Collier, an excellent though temperamental writer who over
the next several months supplied Heston and Seltzer with the
beginnings of the kind of high-quality film script they had
envisioned.

Meanwhile, Charlton went off to Hawaii for *Diamond Head*
which director Guy Green planned to shoot on the Island of
Kauai where the sun, they said, always shone. Instead, it
rained almost all the time.

Because of past experiences, he began working with Yvette
Mimieux uneasily, wary of any temperamentality that might
arise. None did: Mimieux proved to be a pro. But it was not
an easy film for Heston to work on – the weather played
havoc with the schedule. The monotony was broken, however, by a couple of weekend visits from the family.

The picture was completed back in Los Angeles, but Charlton was soon back in the air again, heading for Madrid to do
*55 Days at Peking* under the direction of Nicholas Ray. How
he allowed himself to get involved in this disastrous enterprise is a mystery which must still elude him.

It had all begun with Samuel Bronston and Anthony Mann
virtually begging him to play the fictitious role of a Roman
general in the historical epic they were planning, *The Fall of
the Roman Empire*. Already Bronston's set designers were
busily engaged in erecting a formidable full-size, three-
dimensional replica of the Roman Forum on the plains of Las

Matas. Herman Citron was anxious for him to do the film, but Charlton just wasn't satisfied with the half-finished script they presented to him. However, he read through the research material they provided him with.

He considered the project for several weeks, but the dissatisfaction he felt over *El Cid* finally convinced him to stay clear. Almost the moment he gave them a firm no, Nick Ray came on the scene, per Bronston's orders, with a treatment for *55 Days at Peking*, the story of the Chinese Boxer rebellion. Here was a period of history Charlton had not yet explored and he was immediately intrigued by the concept, even though there was no script ready. He also had an inclination to work for Ray who was a very workmanlike, often sensitive director. He'd recently made *King of Kings*, the story of Jesus Christ, for Bronston. Obviously, Heston had not seen *King of Kings*, a respectable biblical film but far inferior to *El Cid*. Had Charlton done so, he would have recognized that Mann's flair for historical drama and spectacle was superior to Ray's. It was a bad case of misjudgement when Heston agreed to do the Boxer film, basing his decision purely on Nicholas Ray's record as a director.

As soon as Heston said yes to *Peking*, Bronston ordered his set designers to transform the half-completed Roman Forum into late-nineteenth-century Peking. Charlton really should have gone with the *Roman Empire* picture. Not only did it prove to be a better film than *Peking*, but it was also a lot less trouble to make. But at the time there was no way that Chuck could envisage the calamity that would befall him and all those involved in *55 Days at Peking*.

# 17

# Boxers and Baptists

JUST PRIOR TO HEADING OUT TO MADRID, HESTON GOT A sudden offer from George Stevens to play John the Baptist in *The Greatest Story Ever Told*. At first he reasoned that he just didn't want to play another prophet or make another epic. But there were several attractions – it would be shot entirely in America; it was a cameo role and therefore he wouldn't have to bear the burden of the whole film; and George Stevens was not a director to turn down without serious consideration.

After weighing up the pros and cons, he accepted Stevens's offer. When I asked him what clinched it for him, he said,

> Primarily I chose to do it to work with Stevens. It was also a very good part. I think out of all those parts, Jesus aside – and Jesus is really unplayable – the Baptist was really the best. All that lovely stuff screaming about the mountains shall be brought low.

Heston loves good meaty dialogue, and although his role would be brief – it's the only film in which he ever got killed off before the intermission – the dialogue was superb stuff.

Unfortunately, there was still no script for *55 Days at Peking*. 'How can we defend Peking without dialogue?' asked Heston. Suddenly, even before arriving in Spain, the prospects for *Peking* were looking decidedly gloomy. To his total dismay, he received word that Ava Gardner was to be his co-star. He just couldn't see her playing a Russian countess, and he kicked up a fuss. There began a desperate search to find a replacement, but by the time Heston had arrived in Spain it seemed almost unsolvable. The European distributors said they wanted Gardner in the picture. Heston wanted Melina Mercouri. For weeks the battle went on until, finally, Heston, who had casting approval, gave up and let them cast

115

who they wanted, which was Ava Gardner.

Still the script was unshootable, although all the production values were first class. The costumes were beautiful and the fabulous set of Peking was awesome. Heston was delighted with his other co-star, David Niven, portraying the British Ambassador.

Charlton found it immensely hard to warm to Ava Gardner. When she attacked the script and her part, he found himself curiously defending a screenplay he knew was nowhere near good. But Nick Ray seemed to have the gift of soothing her, especially on the set where she displayed a surprising sense of insecurity.

As shooting progressed at a very slow pace, Heston and Niven found themselves making up most of their own dialogue to compensate for the trivial lines they had been given. Finally, Charlton convinced them to bring Ben Barzman in to rewrite what Philip Yordan and Bernard Gordon had already written. But the big bug-bear was Gardner. She began disappearing, insisting she was too sick to work. And when she did work, she invariably turned up late. Inevitably, Nick Ray came to the conclusion they'd made a big mistake, and he began cutting her part down, in some cases giving important establishing lines of hers to other actors. It was also decided to kill her character off long before the picture was at an end.

The tremendous pressures heaped upon Ray in having to deal with a temperament like Gardner while dealing simultaneously with such a gigantic production took their terrible toll on him. He suffered a heart attack and was knocked out of the picture altogether. After hospitalization he fortunately recovered, but he never worked again. The direction of the picture was taken over by Andrew Marton whose primary responsibility was to shoot the second unit sequences. Guy Green, at Heston's insistence, also came out to help, directing the final remaining major scenes, allowing Marton to concentrate on the battle footage. Consequently, the best thing about the film is its action, while everything else falls completely flat.

Green seemed to succeed in getting Gardner to respond and she behaved more professionally. He was soon able to wind up her scenes. From that time on, Heston worked frantically with both first and second units both night and day for a week. It was a depressing experience. Heston had gone in with high hopes for an interesting period film, and ended up slaving away just to finish the picture in the most efficient and professional way possible. But he knew that not even the most skilful of editing could possibly save the final result.

At least he had John the Baptist to look forward to.

Page, Arizona just had to be the bleakest place he'd filmed in since the Sinai Peninsula. George Stevens had secured an area of desert behind the Glen Canyon Dam, among rocks and arroyos which would be flooded as soon as *The Greatest Story Ever Told* was finished.

At least Chuck was able to sleep at home for this one. He'd get up about five AM and catch the plane which would take him out to the film camp built of aluminium huts. At the end of each day he'd be whisked back to Los Angeles to the bosom of his family, determined not to work away on an overseas location again for a long, long time.

His first day of shooting was hardly as frantically paced as the filming had been on *Peking*. At one point Stevens seemed to disappear after doing one brief shot. Then Heston saw him some forty yards away, sitting on a rock, deep in thought. No one dared approach him. He stayed like that for three hours, and then returned and did the shot again. It was virtually impossible to tell what he did differently this time, but at least Heston knew that Stevens wasn't going to put anything on film until he'd convinced himself there was no better way to shoot it.

Charlton found himself spending a long time down in the Colorado River, baptizing people. They had begun shooting in the autumn of 1962 and they were still at it when winter came upon them.

For hours at a time, Heston stood up to his waist in freezing cold water, crying repentance to the heathen, and finally baptizing Max Von Sydow, who gave the most beautiful portrayal ever of the Saviour.

Charlton told me:

Baptizing Max was a painful experience. He's a lovely man and a marvellous actor, and I loved playing the scene with him. But we shot that down in the Colorado River in November, and that bloody water was an average temperature of 42 degrees. And that is *cold*!

I was standing up to my waist in it all day long, dipping people. We used a lot of local people to play the baptizees, and George shot quite slowly and meticulously. Often they'd be waiting all day long for their chance to be baptized, and they were looking forward to being in a scene.

It was lovely to see when it finally came to their turn. They'd step into the water and you'd see this expression of what I trust came across as spiritual ecstasy on their faces! And when I actually dipped them, they'd come up semiconscious. I said to George at the time, 'George, if the Jordan River had been as cold as the Colorado, Christianity would never have gotten off the ground!'

There were footprints in the snow; footprints of children, and tracks of sledges behind the house running down the hill which Charlton had sledged down as a boy. St Helen was the place to be at Christmas so that Charlton could walk Lydia through the woods to enjoy the wintry scene, even if all the presents had been left back at Coldwater.

John Collier had sent more pages from *The Lovers* to his St Helen lodge. It gave Charlton immense pleasure to wallow both in memories of his childhood and in the high-quality writing which Collier was providing. He began to feel that *The Lovers* could be a picture to remember.

Returning to the role of John the Baptist, he suddenly found himself in the curious position of being told by George Stevens to direct a single scene in which Herod's men come to arrest the Baptist.

'But what do you want me to do with it, George?' Chuck asked, somewhat flabbergasted.

'Whatever you want,' replied Stevens.

Heston told me, 'That was a heady feeling to have George Stevens say, "I really have to get back to the set. *You* direct this scene." God knows, it was a simple enough scene.'

With his work on *The Greatest Story Ever Told* finally finished, he was free to concentrate a little more on trying to get
his pet project off the ground. Walter Selzter convinced him
that *The Lovers* was not a title to hook a studio. He came up
with a suggestion: *The War Lord*. Heston and Seltzer did the
rounds to all the major studios with their screen property.
Not since *The Private War of Major Benson* had Charlton
worked so actively in setting up his own production,
although his name would not appear on the credits in any
other capacity than as the star of the picture.

Meanwhile, other matters continued to take up time and
space in the thoughts and actions of Heston. Producer Julian
Blaustein wanted him to portray General Gordon in his
planned epic *Khartoum*, but Charlton was adamant that he
didn't want – indeed, didn't *need* – another blockbuster just
yet.

He was also caught up in a civil rights march that caused his
earlier excursion in Oklahoma to pale into virtual insignificance. This time he was marching with a huge group of
actors, musicians and other artists who called themselves
'The Arts Group'. It seemed only natural, with so many
heroic parts to his credit, that Heston should be immediately
elected chairman of the group. Their plan was to march in
Washington up the Mall towards the Lincoln Memorial
where speeches would be made.

It was a curious position for Charlton to find himself in
because under normal circumstances he opposed any form of
group action. But this time he was one of almost a hundred
famous names including Paul Newman, Harry Belafonte,
Burt Lancaster, Marlon Brando, James Garner and Sidney
Poitier.

As chairman, Heston countered many efforts to turn the
march into an extreme militant rally. Some wanted to chain
themselves to the Thomas Jefferson Memorial on Pennsylvania Avenue. Charlton made his point loud and clear. 'We
live in a country where we have the right to do this kind of
thing,' he told them, 'and if I go then we're going to do it the
way the book says to do it.' On the big day during the
summer of 1963, there were almost a quarter of a million
people moving up the Mall like the Children of Israel in *The*

*Ten Commandments*, only this time the man who played Moses was lost somewhere in the middle of it all. Stirring speeches were made at the Lincoln Memorial – the most stirring of all being Martin Luther King's 'I have a dream...'

As the march finished and people began to drift home, Charlton passed by the Thomas Jefferson monument, and felt that this outstanding President of the United States would have approved. Five months later the Civil Rights Act was passed by Congress in consequence of that day.

It was only appropriate that Heston's next acting job should be portraying Thomas Jefferson himself in the television play *The Patriots*, which was not sent out live since the Golden Age of television was now passed.

Still *The War Lord* hung in the air, and as autumn rolled in, the project seemed no nearer to getting on film. Heston has noted that the films you care about the most are often the most painstakingly difficult to set up. He could, however, console himself with the fact that *55 Days at Peking*, despite its banality, was holding up reasonably well at the box-office, though it was not the success *El Cid* had been. He couldn't help feeling partly responsible for the way *Peking* had turned out and, whether he realized it or not, he would have better served, and been better served by, *The Fall of the Roman Empire* if he'd had to make a choice between the two Bronston films.

# 18

# Agonies and Ecstasies

In the darkened screening room, Charlton watched a surprisingly good western, *Ride the High Country* – 'surprising' since the distributors, MGM, hadn't known quite what to do with it, and had virtually thrown it away. Nevertheless, it won much acclaim, including a prize at the Venice Film Festival.

What really impressed Heston was the assured direction of Sam Peckinpah, convincing him that here was the man to make a fine film out of his next project, still unwritten – *Major Dundee*.

What Heston couldn't have known, of course, was that *Ride the High Country*, despite later successes, would remain Peckinpah's most accomplished and enjoyable film. It was also very different from *Dundee*. Producer Jerry Bresler and Columbia were going to spend a lot of money on *Major Dundee* whereas the earlier film had been made on a shoestring.

Nevertheless, with Heston's approval, *Major Dundee* got under way with Peckinpah directing. From the outset there was much enthusiasm from all quarters, and Charlton believed that this picture could be the very first to examine seriously certain aspects of the American Civil War. The only problem was, his concept, based on the unfinished script, was not harmonious with the ideas that everyone else had. Columbia really wanted an expensive cowboys'n'injuns picture, while Peckinpah envisioned the story of a group of men whose circumstances dictate their violent actions. Already, the seeds of *The Wild Bunch* were taking root in the mind of Peckinpah.

Set during the civil war, *Major Dundee* opens with Heston as Dundee, the warden of a POW camp, coming upon the aftermath of an Indian attack in which children are taken captive. He subsequently takes off after the Indians in an effort to prove that he is still capable of command, taking with him Confederate prisoners including their own leader, Captain Tyreen, an old personal enemy. Dundee knows that when the mission is over, Tyreen is bent on killing him.

The story sounded good coming from Jerry Bresler, but when the script finally arrived at Coldwater Canyon, Charlton was quite appalled by it. He explains:

> One of the mistakes I hope I learned not to make again in the preparation of *Major Dundee*, is never, never start shooting without a complete script. Part of this was the fault of a very inadequate writer who was on at first and

worked for several months and was unable to produce anything even remotely shootable.
    This forced the studio into a five-month postponement,
after which they told Sam Peckinpah to write it. So he
finally undertook it and did his best, but we still weren't
ready when the second shooting date came up.

    Finally, in February 1964, *Major Dundee* began shooting
down in Durango in Mexico from a far from satisfactory
script. The intention was to improve on the written material
on the set. This was a process that had worked brilliantly with
*Ben-Hur* but had failed miserably on *55 Days at Peking*. Charlton was determined that this was a situation he would never
find himself in again.
    As filming commenced, it soon became apparent that this
would not be a pleasurable experience. There were tremendous pressures on everyone which increased as filming progressed, and relationships on the set became strained. Heston
told me: '*Dundee* was very tough to make because Sam Peckinpah was a complicated man. He's an extremely talented
man and you may, depending on your definition of the word,
call him a genius if you will. But he's not an easy man to work
for.'
    Heston had tremendous respect for Peckinpah, and by and
large they worked well together, but Peckinpah was shooting
way over budget and the Columbia brass started to get itchy.
They put the screws on him to speed things up, but, determined to do it all his way, he continued to work at his own
pace. But the pressure took its toll, and in one heated
moment, Heston very nearly ran Peckinpah down with his
horse!
    It happened when Peckinpah told Heston to bring his troop
of cavalry towards the camera at a trot. This he did, but Peckinpah cried, 'Cut! That's too damn slow, Chuck. I said bring
'em in at a canter.' Heston's blood boiled, and he spurred his
horse at high speed towards Peckinpah, pulling up just short
of running him down. 'I'll bring them in any damn way you
want,' he cried, 'but damn it, you said trot, not canter.'
    Heston has a theory about this peculiar behaviour which
Peckinpah displayed from time to time: 'He had a curious

compulsion to make people mad at him. He didn't feel he'd
involved you unless he made you mad at him, and he finally
did. But I didn't count it as a victory. It was a loss.'

As the difficulties increased on *Major Dundee*, Heston's
shadow became ever more ominous. He exercised what authority he had and grew stronger. According to director
Andrew V. McLaglen, this has much to do with portraying
people like Moses and Ben-Hur, which is debatable, but it
was evident, and Richard Harris was determined not to bend
the knee. He says:

> Heston's the only man who could drop out of a cubic moon
> – he's so square We never got on. The trouble with him is
> he doesn't think he's just a hired actor, like the rest of us.
> He thinks he's the entire production. He used to sit there in
> the mornings and clock us in with a stop-watch.
>
> I got sick of this, so I brought an old alarm clock and
> hung it around my neck and set it to go off at the moment
> he walked in one day.
>
> 'I don't find that amusing,' he said. 'Well,' I said, 'you
> know what you can do, don't you?'

According to Heston, Harris was not the most professional
of actors, taking delight, it seemed, in being stricken from
time to time with one ailment or another. Of course, Heston
judges the world by his own standard of professionalism
which, according to many assistant directors and producers,
is extremely high. He makes no apology for this. He told me:

> Shouting and tantrums and bursting into tears and slam-
> ming doors and throwing chairs is, at least in my view,
> enormously counter-productive, and to a degree I cannot
> tolerate it and I won't tolerate it. If that sounds hard-nosed,
> I mean it to sound hard-nosed.
>
> I am delighted to hear that assistant directors and pro-
> ducers and people I work with say, 'Chuck takes coming to
> work on time very seriously,' because I *do* take coming to
> work on time and knowing lines very seriously. I've been
> at this trade a long time, and I think Spencer Tracey defined
> screen acting better than anyone else. He said, 'Come to

work on time, know your lines, don't bump into the furniture, and *then* you can work.'

Whatever the problems were between Heston and Harris,
Heston maintains that, while strained, their working relationship was not a virtual feud. 'Richard is very much the
*professional Irishman*,' he said. 'I found him a somewhat erratic
personality and an occasional pain in the posterior. But we
certainly never feuded.'

In fact, he seems to go out of his way to avoid confrontations on the set. He told me, 'If you become impatient or
angry with the people you are working with, you're only
hurting your work. Some people seem to thrive on a certain
amount of common drama and racing around and screaming
on the set. I don't like that. The work's hard enough to do as
it is. I don't want people arguing.'

As the pressure increased and the budget soared ever
higher, a peculiar thing happened. Columbia were just about
to pull the plug on Peckinpah. Undoubtedly, at that time
Heston's status in the business was much higher than Peckinpah's, and nothing Peckinpah could say would change Columbia's minds. So Charlton stepped into the situation and,
although in this particular picture he had no legal rights to
interfere with the actual production, he convinced the studio
to leave Sam out there with his unit for a little while longer. A
little later, feeling guilty at overstepping his authority, Charlton called up Mike Frankovich, the boss at Columbia, and
told them that he was willing to waive his entire fee of
$300,000 because he had made the studio compromise in a
way that under more normal circumstances, Heston would
never have approved of. 'That's a nice gesture, Chuck,' said
Frankovich, 'but we wouldn't dream of taking your salary.'

He certainly felt relieved to still have his fee, since on this
picture there would be no share of the profits. Herman
Citron, however, told him that the studio would rethink and
accept his offer. Charlton assured him that everything was all
right. But Citron proved correct. Heston suddenly found
himself making one of the most difficult pictures of his life for
free.

From that moment on, things got progressively worse.

There were representatives from Columbia on the set every day. There were certain scenes they wanted eliminated from the shooting schedule to save time and money. Every lunch hour was spent in heated discussion between the studio brass and Peckinpah and Heston, each contingent putting their case. Peckinpah with Heston's support managed to convince them to allow them to shoot the scenes in question, but there was still arguing between them in the evenings back at the hotel, often ending only at two or three in the morning, with a 5 AM call facing them for the next day's work.

Making *Major Dundee* was sometimes a painful experience, and even dangerous. Earlier on in production Heston fell off his horse and damaged his elbow. The doctor told him to rest up for two weeks. 'Like hell,' said Heston. 'I'll be back on the set tomorrow.' He concealed his arm beneath the serape he wore for certain scenes, determined that Peckinpah would not find out and then start shooting around him.

It was an act of pride on Heston's part. He told me, 'I've never missed a day's work or even a day's rehearsal and I'm very proud of it, as a matter of fact.'

Towards the end of shooting, in true heroic fashion, Chuck insisted on doing what the stunt men call a 'cossack drag' – a favourite for cowboy films whereby the stunt man gets dragged along the ground with one foot caught in the horse's stirrup. But for this scene, it was to be in a river. Heston pulled the horse over in the water, allowing his foot to stay caught in the stirrup. It was a tricky and momentarily potentially dangerous act that didn't quite come off. As he told me, 'There were guys around me and one of them pulled the horse out of the river. If the horse had gotten away I suppose I would have had a difficult time.'

He was relieved when the whole enterprise was at an end. It had been a pretty horrendous experience. Today, with rather sardonic humour, Heston looks back on it as a feat of endurance and survival.

If you ask anyone that goes through tough locations, I'm sure they'll tell you that there was a certain sense of delight at having survived them. You tend to say, 'You remember how it was on *Dundee* down in Mexico and that damned river when we couldn't eat the food and there was goat hide on the meat!' But you say it with delight, and you say, 'But they didn't get me that time!'

It's kind of an horrendous game. The best way to survive is to say, 'Okay, you son-of-a-bitch, you want me to come back at seven o'clock in the morning – I'll *come* back at seven. You think I can't do another take – I'll *do* another take. You want me to change into another wardrobe and take off the make-up – all right, I'll go and take off the beard and make-up.' There's that kind of defiant feeling to it as well.

With the picture complete, Columbia took it right away from Peckinpah and so many of the scenes which Heston and Peckinpah had fought to include in the filming went. When Charlton finally saw the finished picture, he was dismayed. Peckinpah maintained that had he been given a free hand all the way down the line, he would have produced the film they had all hoped for. Heston disagrees.

I'm not certain that even if Sam had been allowed to cut it the way he wanted to that *Dundee* could ever have been the picture he had in mind. It certainly would have been better than the film we have, but it was constantly subjected to controversy – the way we shot it and what was to be shot. I would have to concede to the studio's position that the film was flawed. The only trouble is that they tried to cut it into something simpler and more routine and I don't think they succeeded in making it into the film they had in mind either.

And we all had different films in mind. I was very interested, and remained interested, in making a film about the American Civil War. It demonstrated the strength and flexibility of the Union, in that the United States could survive the bloody trauma. It's not a good film in any terms.

He paced over the steps he had trodden six years before on that great Roman circus where he had spent months driving his chariot to victory. Even compared to *Major Dundee, Ben-*

*Hur* was still the toughest picture he'd ever done. Now here he was in Rome, just one month after finishing his film for Peckinpah, all set to play Michelangelo in *The Agony and the Ecstasy*.

There had barely been four weeks in which to spend time on his Coldwater ridge, winding down from the months spent in Mexico, and preparing for the months ahead in Rome. He did so want to be home more often – so why was he here?

From the moment that he read the screenplay of *The Agony and the Ecstasy* which Philip Dunne had adapted from Irving Stone's novel, he knew it just had to be the best script he'd ever seen. The offer to play the part had come from Twentieth Century-Fox, who seemed willing to pour millions into the project, despite the disaster that had just befallen them with *Cleopatra*.

This picture just reeked of class. He hoped they could get Fred Zinnemann to direct, and maybe Laurence Olivier to play the Pope. He immediately immersed himself in research on the man who painted the Sistine Chapel.

However, it quickly became apparent to him that it was not so much the written material in which he would find the Michelangelo whom he would portray. He would find him in his statues, such as Moses and David.

By the time Heston was in Rome for the actual filming, the director was not Zinnemann, but Carol Reed, and instead of Olivier for the Pope, they had Rex Harrison.

Portraying Michelangelo was very quickly becoming one of Heston's most extraordinary and satisfying acting experiences. Just the make-up alone called for Heston to make his nose look even more broken than it already was. To achieve this he stuck little bits of rubber up his nostrils and added a little paint. With a closely trimmed beard and an authentic Florentine haircut, he emerged looking remarkably like the available portraits of Michelangelo.

He continued to read letters and biographies, trying not to lounge too lazily in the luxurious villa they gave him for the duration, but what really did it for him was to climb the scaffold that the Vatican had graciously allowed to be erected in the Sistine Chapel, and there to imagine the torment and anguish that Michelangelo suffered with every stroke of his brush to complete the world's greatest painting in four agonizing years.

In his spare time he walked around the seemingly ageless streets where Michelangelo had once trod, and went back again and again to see the statues. Even before a single camera rolled, Charlton Heston had come as close to Michelangelo as to any character he had ever portrayed before.

Obviously, there was no way they could film inside the actual Sistine Chapel, and so a complete replica was constructed at the studios in Rome. Of course, Heston didn't paint the whole ceiling himself. That was achieved by carefully photographing the whole ceiling in stages and printing them full-scale on to their set ceiling. They were able to cover great sections of the painting with panels, revealing those sections as the film progressed until the whole ceiling was on display in all its glorious, painful, ecstatic splendour.

After the agonies of making *Major Dundee* and *55 Days at Peking*, this work was pure ecstasy, but Heston felt that Reed was too often too kind, not pushing Heston to the limits that he should have been reaching for. And Rex Harrison wasn't the easiest man to work with, for his was a temperament that caused a few headaches. Certainly there was nothing that could stop Charlton from enjoying this rare movie acting experience.

The critics didn't share his enthusiasm. They slated the picture, and it was also a commercial flop, which astounded him. He felt he'd never acted better in any film, and he seemed to have really got under the skin of Michelangelo. But his leading lady in the film, Diane Cilento, is critical of his interpretation of the part.

'He refused to believe probably the most well-documented case of homosexuality in history,' she told me. 'Well, it was just a great joke because he wasn't going to play him like that.'

She also found it a hilarious experience acting with him. 'It was really funny because he was so enormous that when we stood in shot together, I came up to his navel. So I had to wear these huge great clumping boots!'

As to the failure of the film, she says, 'It was just a rather odd picture – one of those big epic things, and everybody knew it was really Charlton Heston and Rex Harrison and me and a few other people in Rome painting the Sistine Chapel. 'And it wasn't the greatest plot in the world!'

# 19

# The Lice and Loves of Michelangelo

THE HEADLINE SCREAMED OUT AT THE ITALIAN READERSHIP, 'I Pulci di Michelangelo' – 'The Lice of Michelangelo'! And the photographs strewn across the front page of Lo Specchio proved its case; empty bottles littered the floor of the villa where the Hestons had stayed during the filming of The Agony and the Ecstasy, broken crockery lay strewn across the floor, chairs were overturned. There were, according to the publication, lice all over the house. It went on to report how Charlton Heston and his wife had left their sumptuous villa in this disgusting state, proving that the man who played Moses and John the Baptist was, after all, no saint at all.

It was, to say the least, a frame-up.

Lydia was terribly hurt by the scandalous story. Charlton even considered suing the magazine. But through it all Chuck somehow managed to laugh at the whole thing. Lydia explained:

An Italian magazine had gone into the house we'd rented, put the pictures askew, thrown chairs down, pulled the cloth off the table in the dining room, then taken a photograph and said that was how we'd left it. It was a complete fabrication and I was ready to go over there and do battle.

But Chuck thought it was funny!

It was the very first time that Heston's name had been

linked with anything even vaguely scandalous. It's always acted against his becoming showily popular, as far as gossip columnists are concerned, that he never seems to put a foot out of place. Frank Sinatra once said of Heston, 'That guy Heston has to watch it. If he's not careful, he'll get actors a good name.' Charlton is slightly self-derisive about his own image:

I'm too dull, square and protestant – in the philosophical not the religious sense – to be a big popular public figure; a beloved figure. I'm not a public drunk. I've only had one wife. My kids aren't runaways. It's not what people expect.

I go along in a square way and it's not very interesting. People don't find a big public flaw in me and they seem to need it, not just from me, but from anyone who's had success and attention.

Some people do jerky things because it doesn't occur to them that their behaviour will be reported by the press and television. I've fallen into a behaviour pattern because everything I say or do is going on the record, and I want to have a good record. Frank Sinatra and Elizabeth Taylor make a lot of news. That just isn't my style.

Actors who are public figures are given a curious indulgence. They can get drunk, beat their wives or divorce them, and they will be forgiven – indeed, rather applauded, because the public likes to have someone who can get away with doing the things they themselves can't do or dare not do. The perfect death for an actor is Marilyn Monroe's, naked on the floor of a house in Beverly Hills in which the rent is not paid, with an empty bottle of sleeping pills and no friends. She picks up the phone and nobody comes.

See, really, that's where you pay off. You have to pay the piper. And, therefore, I'm not a very satisfactory public star.

Audiences like stars who seem to suffer, who are disappointed in love, always on the brink of some personal disaster. Well, I'm not like that, and I'm not inclined to break up my home in order to get a fan following.

Indeed, there are far more sobering reasons why Heston's home life has been so stable. His own experience as a child in a broken home has left its mark on him, only now he is the parent with two children of his own to think of.

If parents realized how deeply divorce cuts into the hearts of children, there probably wouldn't be such a frightening divorce rate in the country. Sometimes, I imagine, divorce seems the only sane solution to an unhappy pair. I do think, however, it is imperative that somehow the natural tie with both parents should not be cut.

What you do with a child always means infinitely more than material gifts. I've never forgotten this. That's why I spend as much time as I can with Fray and Holly. I've taken Fray on as many of my location trips as I can, because I remember the thrill a boy gets out of being with his father.

Fray lived in Spain for seven months the first time I filmed there, learned the language and something of the people. When we returned to Rome to film *The Agony and the Ecstasy*, Fray reminisced about the ten months he previously lived on the Appian Way during the making of *Ben-Hur!*

A father shouldn't have to pretend to be perfect. And he doesn't have to be profound. He just has to communicate.

In a business where the divorce rate is so high – just try counting the stars who haven't been divorced – the Hestons seem to stand as sturdy as the granite performance of Heston's Moses. But Charlton is quick to point out that their marriage is not all that unusual.

It would be pointless and less than truthful to say that we live in absolute bliss every minute of the day. That would be impossible for anyone. You've got to learn not to think, when you argue, 'Oh God, that does it. I can't go on with this.'

You've got to conquer the bumps and emotional bruises. You've got to take it that the other person is doing his or her best, and to be as ready to find excuses for the other person as you are to find excuses for yourself. It needs a lot of working at – but it can bear wonderful results.

Marriage requires some attention, and kids marrying at nineteen – as Lydia and I did – imagine it's going to be one long honeymoon. It isn't.

Lydia and Charlton have obviously learned to be tolerant of each other and cope with each other's quirks. In some ways they are incompatible, yet they seem to have worked out a formula for coping with their differences, or simply putting up with them.

One such thing is packing, and the Hestons do a lot of that. Chuck hates it. 'I get tense if we're getting ready to take a trip,' he says, 'because the sheer business of packing irritates me.' He leaves all that up to Lydia. She has to cope with that, as she does with some of his virtues which she perhaps lacks.

She says:

Organization, tidiness, and punctuality – he's very precise with his papers, and never late. I'm the opposite. Nothing is ever where I put it. Not that *I* mind things on the floor. But I mind that Chuck minds me for *my* things on the floor. I'm always late, and when I turn up he's got his eyes glued to his watch.

So how does she explain their success as husband and wife?

'I think essentially it's a matter of wanting to be married,' she says. 'I think you have to find a man who is genuinely interested in being married. Then it works very easily.'

Perhaps the biggest problem that they have had to overcome is the pressures that are put upon all of them because of Charlton's work.

He says:

Of course my work intrudes enormously on my personal life, and that takes time from my wife and from my children that I wish I didn't have to take. But they react with understanding. My work is the centre of my life, and they understand that. We're quite cohesive about it.

He has, however, learned to control how a great deal of his time gets used up, because for him work is very often more than just making films or performing in plays. It also involves publicizing his products which often results in world whistle-stop tours that cannot always include his family.

I suppose I feel myself being 'used up' in my public time. So I don't go to parties a great deal when I'm at home, because I associate them with work. When I'm touring for a picture there are receptions and parties. If a friend has a *première* I'll go to it, and there'll probably be a party afterwards. Or maybe it's a charity affair. I'm not blasé. Some of them are great fun. But it's *work*.

But it isn't just his desire to spend as much time with his family as he can that keeps him from attending all the typical Hollywood celebrity shindigs. There is one very basic aspect of Heston's nature that, despite the public image, has not changed.

People find it very hard to believe when he says:

I'm a very shy person. It's true. But I've been a public actor for so long, for most of my life, that I've arrived at a kind of a way to behave in my public life.

I'm a very private person, and when I'm in the tiny part of my life that is private, I never go out and I never see people I haven't known for a long time. I meet new people very reluctantly and very shyly.

Of course I do interviews. When I started performing, I was very shy about doing them and wasn't very good at it. Now I do them quite well because I've learned how to.

Charlton Heston, the private man, the public actor – he never refers to himself as a *star* – is a man at odds with himself, yet has discovered how to bridge the gap between the part of him that's shy with the part that has to go out and perform. The little boy who lived in St Helen has not changed too drastically. But the misfit from Chicago has learned how to cope with every facet of his life, but on his own terms. A misfit no more, he has built for himself a castle on a canyon and put up an invisible barrier that prevents anyone, except his very best friends and of course his family, from knowing the real Charlton Heston too well. And that barrier, as I would later discover, is his own skill as an actor to project through performance, even in interviews, a public personality that isn't necessarily the private one.

# 20

# The Extraordinary Man

AFTER SO MANY MONTHS OVER THE PAST YEAR WORKING ON such far-flung locations as Mexico and Rome, it was pure joy to make a film completely in California at last. The fact that he was making *The War Lord* at all was enough to excite him, because it was now more than two years since he first set in motion the preparation to film Leslie Stevens's beautiful play *The Lovers*.

Much of the time had been spent in fashioning a screenplay, which John Collier had slowly and meticulously done, but the hardest part was finding a studio to back it. Finally, Universal gave him the go-ahead, but they were more interested in making the film as spectacular as their limited budget would allow, and they wanted a much happier ending than the one in the original script, which had Heston's character, an eleventh-century Norman knight, killed off. They put Millard Kaufman to work on the ending and Charlton's old live-TV pal Franklin Schaffner took the helm as director. Charlton worked closely with Walter Seltzer in setting up the whole production, but he preferred not to have his name credited as co-producer.

Crucial to the success of the film was the casting of the young maiden whom the War Lord takes on her wedding night, initially out of passion, resulting in a strange and deep love between them. Young Rosemary Forsyth, twenty-years-old and the veteran of just one previous picture, was chosen. Supporting roles went to Richard Boone, Maurice Evans, Guy Stockwell and Henry Wilcoxon.

Location shooting took place in the marshlands of Marysville substituting for Belgium, and then they returned to the back lot of Universal Studios where an authentic-looking Norman tower had been erected for the spectacular battle scenes. It was now winter and the usual Californian sun had disappeared, making it much colder than usual, helping to give the night-time scenes a remarkable chilling effect.

Joe Cannutt was directing the second unit, as he would do on virtually all of Heston's films, and with basically little more than a handful of extras, he made the battle scenes extremely effective, though nowhere near as lavish as the *El Cid* battles. But then intimacy was what Charlton had hoped for, although he was battling somewhat against Universal's determination, understandably, to make this a commercial proposition.

The filming went comparatively smoothly, and it was only after the film was in the can that the trouble began. As had happened so often with Heston's films, the studio decided to take the director off the project and allow the editing to be supervised by someone else. Schaffner had already cut the film the way he wanted it and Heston was delighted with it. But Universal were adamant and legally able to do what they wanted with the finished product.

*The War Lord* remains an exceptional film, but one which Heston was disappointed in because his dream, which had been the same as Seltzer's and Schaffner's, had been shattered. 'I thought the way Frank cut it was just right,' he says, 'just about what was needed. But then after we had all gone home, the studio cut it again. Their cutting spoiled a film that was nearly exactly what those who had created it had in mind.'

That an actor is always subject to the whims of so many others is a fact of life which Charlton accepts. But on the stage where it is really 'actor's country' he knew he could make a play stand or fall. Following *The War Lord* he and Lydia did *A Man For All Seasons* in Chicago which proved to be a huge personal hit for Charlton. For the first time ever, he felt the magic that comes following a performance when the audience literally rose and screamed for him.

Immediately after *A Man For All Seasons*, he was off over-seas yet again, this time to Cairo and London for *Khartoum*. At first he had been reluctant to accept the role of General Gordon because it was to be another spectacular epic, but the screenplay by Robert Ardrey was arguably the best screen-play he'd ever read, superseding even *The Agony and the Ecstasy*.

At his own suggestion, the part of the Mahdi was offered to Laurence Olivier, who accepted, but Charlton was unhappy with the choice of director, Basil Dearden.

He told me:

> I think I would have to say that *Khartoum* is the only picture I've made which I consider a very good picture that I didn't think was very well directed. It did have a superb script and had a very gifted producer, Julian Blaustein, and it also had a very good cast. But perhaps the key there was the quality of the script.

It was a challenging part for Charlton, since he had to learn to speak with the kind of accent that a Victorian British Gen-eral would have used. He was immensely successful, and Heston was easily accepted by British audiences. In fact, Gordon of Khartoum remains one of Heston's finest per-formances. It was a part that stirred him greatly, and in many ways was not too unlike El Cid or Moses or many of the other parts that he had portrayed in that they were all extraordinary men who touched millions of people in their actions. Heston says:

> I believe very much in the power of the extraordinary man to move the world. And certainly Gordon was such a man, a remarkable man with the kind of curiously simple re-ligious, almost driven fanaticism which seems to have sur-faced in the history of England when it's needed.
>
> I think it's true what Gordon says about the extraordi-nary man. He says, 'I have learned never to be afraid of death but always to be afraid of failure.'

*Khartoum* was a great success in Britain, but the American audiences were most reluctant to take it to their bosoms. And that fear of failure entered Heston's life. *The War Lord* had proved to be a commercial failure, and *The Agony and the Ecstasy* was not exactly pulling them in, but perhaps what concerned Chuck more was the way in which the films were received by the critics who were not very kind to any of these pictures. And yet Heston has rarely done better work outside of those three movies.

Putting it down to experience from which to learn, Charlton got on with his next task which was to become the new president of the SAG, an appointment which demonstrated the respect and admiration his peers had for him.

Wounded and dying Seabees and marines lay upon their cots in the advance field hospital, while others were hurriedly carried on stretchers from the helicopter pad straight into the surgical tent. It could almost have been a scene from *M.A.S.H.*, except that this was 1966 before the film or TV series was conceived, and this wasn't Korea, but Vietnam. Charlton stood and watched and talked with them, taking notes of phone numbers and addresses, promising to ring girlfriends, wives, mothers and fathers when he got back.

He hadn't come with dancing girls and songs to sing and jokes to tell. He came only with pride for these men and a hope that somehow his presence there, arranged by the United Service Organizations, might help to boost morale. Also, unlike people like Bob Hope who brought with them rather large entertainment units, he was able to visit some of the more remote outposts who normally saw nothing but death on both sides. When he got back to the States he kept his promise to the boys he'd met and phoned up several hundred friends and relatives of the soldiers. It took Heston days to make all the calls, but he did it gladly, even though under normal circumstances he hated talking to strangers.

Becoming a working actor again, he did *A Man For All Seasons* once more, this time at the Valley Music Theater in Los Angeles, and again he was a big hit in it. It prompted him to chase after the part in the film Fred Zinnemann was planning.

Heston says:

I've played Thomas More twice and was very good in it. It
was one of my best parts. I did something I've almost never
done before or since, which was to write to Freddie Zinnemann and ask for the role in his film. He said, 'Paul Scofield
created the role on stage and I think he deserves it.' And
you can't argue with that. Paul's was a brilliant performance.

Ironically, a year later it was Chuck who, at the Oscar ceremony, took Paul Scofield's name from the envelope and
announced him as Best Actor for his performance as Thomas
More. Still, Charlton and Lydia got to do the play again in
Miami, just a month after doing it in Los Angeles, and he felt
more than satisfied with what he'd achieved with it.

With the exception of one small film role, it was the last
professional acting which Lydia did. Her career had become
very spasmodic, but now it definitely came to a close. 'I have
been so busy that I've never had time to miss my career,' she
says. 'I enjoyed doing A Man For All Seasons with Chuck.
That was marvellous. But there aren't many parts around that
I've wanted to play.' Not surprisingly, she was finding her
time taken up mostly with being a busy mother with two
children to raise. But she adopted a satisfying hobby with
photography which she has since developed into something
of a career.

Having got Thomas More out of his system, Charlton
went to work for the government for a time, when the State
Department sent him off to Australia, Rangoon and Bang-
kok. He visited numerous universities, reading from Australian and American literature, and generally promoting
good relations between America and his host countries.

With his position as SAG president dominating much of
his time, he also found a day to spend in Washington, reading
some Jefferson at Watergate to support the federal pro-
gramme to aid poverty and education.

On his way home he stopped off at Detroit to visit Russ
who'd suffered a series of strokes. While he was there, Russ
had another attack, but Charlton remained optimistic that his

dad would be at Coldwater Canyon for Christmas. The following day Chuck said goodbye to Russ and set off for the
airport to fly to California. While he was in the air, Russ died.
They buried him where he wanted to be left in peace, in
Charlton's beloved St Helen, among the pine trees. Rain was
falling as they put his father into the ground, and then Charlton took Fray deep into the woods where he and Russ had
once explored.

For a while back in his adolescent years, Charlton had lost
his father, and then before going overseas to war, he had
found him again. From that moment, he knew he would
never lose him again. Even now in death, Russ was still his
father, and as long as there were woods and a lake in St Helen,
Charlton knew he would never lose his dad again.


# 21

# Aping Success

OFTEN NOTHING EASES THE PAIN OF BEREAVEMENT LIKE HARD
work, and Charlton was fortunate to have a film to get to
grips with. It was *Counterpoint*, a war-time drama in which he
played a conductor touring with his orchestra in war-torn
Europe. When the orchestra is captured by the Germans,
Heston finds himself involved in a battle of wits with their
captor, played brilliantly by Maximilian Schell.

For the part, Charlton had to learn to conduct under the tu-
ition of Leo Damiani over a period of two months, and he
says that the very thing that attracted him to the film was the
challenge of learning to conduct:

My taste in music has always been classical but, as you rapidly discover, conducting Beethoven on the record player
at one o'clock in the morning in your own home is just not
the same . . . it just isn't the way they do it.
The fact that I'm musically illiterate made it very diffi-

cult. A conductor has to know the score by heart, and you cannot learn a symphonic score unless you can read music really. Fortunately, there was time before shooting began and we managed to find a solution to all these problems.

I would honestly say that learning to pretend to be a conductor was the hardest preparation I've ever done on a film.

He would emerge from each training session soaked in perspiration, but in the process he got to learn to conduct the Beethoven Fifth (or part of it), *Swan Lake* and a touch of Brahms.

In early 1967, following completion of *Counterpoint*, he was summoned to Washington where President L. B. Johnson personally appointed him to the National Council of the Arts. It was an added responsibility which he promised to carry out to the best of his ability, but he still carried the weight of the SAG and was heavily involved at this time to stop the proposed plan to bring studio tourists on to the working sets.

With so much else going on, it's surprising he found time to act. But he had his sights set on a unique little western, *Will Penny*. He explains:

The script was brought to me by Walter Seltzer, and I read it and wanted to do it straight away. I assumed that the man who wrote it, Tom Gries, was a historian or some kind of authority on the old West. But he turned out to be a sports writer who'd never written a western before. I said to Walter that I thought we could get Wyler or George Stevens interested, but he told me that there was a snag. The writer wanted to direct it himself.

I asked what he had directed before – nothing, said Walter. But the script was so good and I wanted so much to do it, that we finally gave in.

It was Heston's own name which prompted Paramount to back the film, and filming began in Bishop, California. Lydia gave her services for just one day in a bit role, although the leading female role went to Joan Hackett whose talent and professionalism delighted Heston. Sadly, Joan Hackett is gone now, never having fulfilled her potential as an actress of note.

Playing the black-hearted villain of the piece was Donald Pleasence who seemed to feel that many of his scenes were cut in deference to Charlton Heston. But he does have an amusing tale to tell:

I played a wild, mad man who shot everyone, had a mistress and tortured Charlton Heston. At the end Heston shoots me with a sawn-off shotgun, knocking me several feet through the air. After we did that scene, Heston said to me, 'That'll teach you to tangle with the leading man.'

What really attracted Heston to the film, beside the quality of the script, was its authenticity. He says:

Will Penny is the opposite of Shane in terms of the protagonist, but he is surrounded by the same realistic environment. Penny is not the mythic Western hero with golden buckskins, fawn-coloured hat, several guns and a beautifully groomed chestnut horse.

I wear a thirty-year-old torn hat, handlebar moustache, and chaps which I stole from an earlier film and have been saving in the back closet. I don't ride a smartly groomed box-stalled horse but one that was purposely corralled outdoors to grow a winter coat.

On location, where everything is of necessity a little farther back such as the microphone boom and the script girl and the cameraman, you have a total environmental surrounding and it is easier to fulfil one of your tasks as an actor which is to persuade yourself that the given circumstances of the story are quite real. I could do this far more readily riding along in the dust stirred up by a thousand head of cattle up on the Orange River Valley where we shot the Will Penny locations, than I could in the totally 'realistic' sets that were constructed on the sound stages at the studio.

Will Penny, the story of an ageing cowboy who feels he's too old to change even for love, remains one of Chuck's personal favourites. It was also, he told me, one of only two films he can recall – *Khartoum* being the other one – on which the script was hardly changed at all.

It was while making *Will Penny* that Charlton, at the coaxing of co-star Bruce Dern, took up running to keep fit. He's hated the professional-runner-turned-actor ever since, he jokes, but since then running daily has become a part of his life.

As had so often happened with a project Charlton cared so much about, the film flopped, despite good reviews. Heston blames the distributors who suddenly thrust the film into a London opening at a live theatre with a cinema screen hastily thrown up. Nobody knew it was there, and Paramount eventually put it out as a double bill with a Tarzan film for kids, which was not the audience the film had been made for.

Heston had not had an unqualified hit since *El Cid*, and he was desperate to find one, and for some time he had in fact been working quietly in the background of a motion picture that would be the very thing he was looking for.

'I want to find something like *King Kong*,' producer Arthur P. Jacobs said. In fact, he was asking just about every literary agent in town, in the hope that someone might have something for him. Then a French agent called him and said, 'I've got something here which is so far out, I don't think you can make it.' He went on to relate the story of a novel by Pierre Boulle called *Monkey Planet*, the story of a world where apes are the masters and humans are the beasts.

Jacobs was ecstatic about the idea. 'I'll buy it,' he cried. 'I gotta have it.'

'I think you're crazy,' said the agent, 'but okay.'

Jacobs spent the next three and a half years trying to persuade a studio to make it, showing them sketches he had commissioned of the apes, but every studio said, 'No way.' 'Then I got Rod Sterling to do the screenplay,' explains Jacobs, 'and went to everybody again – absolute turndown. So then I figured, maybe if I got an actor involved – and I went to Charlton Heston who, in one hour, said yes.'

Jacobs had struck gold, because as Heston explained, 'I was fascinated by it and recognized its clear commercial potential. So I told Arthur what I seldom tell anyone with a project that isn't firmly financed, that I would be interested in doing it.'

Charlton suggested that Frank Schaffner would be the ideal director, so Jacobs managed to hook him also. Then he went back to every studio. At Fox, Richard Zanuck's interest was stirred, but he said, 'This is all fine, but what if people laugh at the make-up?' Jacobs convinced Zanuck to allow them to shoot a test featuring Heston with Edward G. Robinson as the ape Zaius. The test proved Jacobs's point that the apes were not laughable, and Fox gave him the go-ahead, although it was a year after that test that filming proceeded in 1967 in Page, Arizona.

Twentieth Century-Fox is one of Heston's favourite studios, although he has worked there on just a few occasions. Judging the studio by their handling of *Apes*, he says, 'I like the way they work at Fox.' He goes on:

I think Dick Zanuck deserves a great deal of credit for the fact that Fox undertook the picture, because he examined the project and the considerable costs involved. Zanuck had a lot of confidence in Franklin Schaffner, rightly so, as did I, as not only a director of enormous creative ability, but a good captain.

Frank and I have worked together many times and we have a good rapport. I think we understood the part in the same way, and it seemed to fall into place very readily. The major problems in making the film proved to be more technical ones. The creative problems were much more susceptible to ready solution.

There are few science fiction stories which provide any latitude for character change. Taylor's desperate attempts to communicate when he is temporarily speechless is a marvellous acting problem. I must say it's one of the most physically painful parts I've done, as I spend almost every scene either being hit with sticks and stones, or pulled around with a leash about my neck, or squirted with fire hoses, or falling down cliffs.

The film also marked his very first nude scene. Nudity is something Heston has strong feelings about. He says:

If you're just doing it to show a nude broad, I think you usually defeat your own ends. Nudity has to be handled with extreme *selectivity* as well as sensitivity. But sometimes there is a point to be made through nudity. The kind of point we made in *Apes* in the scene in the courtroom where Taylor is stripped naked, is obviously intended to show that to the apes it couldn't mean less, as if they're taking a collar off a dog. I frankly challenge anyone to think of a better way to demonstrate how the apes felt towards the man than to have him stripped and standing there naked.

There was a curious sort of accident in the filming of that scene where the three judges do the 'see no evil, hear no evil, speak no evil' tableau. All the other clichés that the apes use you can justify because theirs was a mimicking culture, and they would logically mimic the speech clichés. But there's no way you could justify *that* – that indeed is a phoney.

When we were shooting the scene, Frank said, 'You know, it would be terribly funny to have a gag of them doing that.' We laughed at it, and he said, 'No, it's a phoney. I shouldn't do it.' I said, 'Why don't you do one just for the dailies,' and he said, 'All right.' So we did it, laughed, and everybody thought it was marvellous, but he didn't want it in the final cut.

Then, somehow, it got in the rough cut, and all the studio echelons saw it and said, 'No, don't change it!' Then they had the first preview, and it was an enormous success. So there it is.

The film was an immediate smash hit, and Fox, deciding there's no business like monkey business, prepared for a sequel, much to Charlton's horror. Resisting all efforts to get him to star in it, he concentrated on a television play, *Elizabeth and Essex*, in late 1967. He was, of course, Essex, opposite Dame Judith Anderson's Elizabeth. It was a prestigious production, directed by George Schaefer, which won an Emmy.

In the meantime, Fox were adamant about aping their success and a script was drawn up for *Beneath the Planet of the Apes*.

Another costume heavy for Heston with the title role of *El Cid* (1961). Here he fights King Alfonso (John Fraser), whose intensely loyal subject the Cid was.

*Major Dundee* (1965) was a project dear to Heston's heart, and a change from his Biblical roles. In *The Greatest Story Ever Told* (1965) he made a cameo appearance as John the Baptist, and spent much time in the almost freezing Colorado River.

Two widely differing roles: as General Gordon in *Khartoum* (1966) and as
George Taylor in *Planet of the Apes* (1969). Heston starred as an American
astronaut who leads a team catapulted through time and space into captivity
on an unidentified planet ruled by apes. (Those shown here are played by
Kim Hunter, Roddy McDowell and Maurice Evans.)

*Julius Caesar* (1970) was a star-studded production in which Heston played Mark Antony, with Jill Bennett as Calpurnia, Robert Vaughn as Casca and Sir John Gielgud as Caesar. In contrast, *Call of the Wild* (1972) was very un-starry – the dogs were scarcely trained!

It was the first film Charlton ever got involved with that he really didn't want to make.

He explains:

I felt a certain obligation to Dick Zanuck about the film. The first one had such an enormous success, both critically and commercially, and of course I was grateful for the part and the material rewards it brought me. They spoke to me as soon as the overwhelming success of the film became evident, about a sequel. I said, 'You know, there is no sequel. There's only one story. You can have further adventures among the monkeys, and it can be an exciting film, but creatively, there is no film.'

Now that comment is in no way intended, as I said to Zanuck, as a criticism of them for making it. A picture that grosses twenty-two million dollars, that has the potential to be spun into one or more sequels obviously gives you a responsibility to your stockholders, and indeed all other movie makers on your lot who will be making films with the profits from that.

It's clear that, in terms of the story, the first one is all there is. Nevertheless, I felt a responsibility to Zanuck and said I'd be happy to do it as a friendly contribution.

In agreeing to do the film, he made them promise to kill him off at the end so that he couldn't possibly appear in any further sequels. This they agreed to, and he even sold them on the idea of blowing up the whole world, probably believing this would bring the series to an end once and for all.

Fox were smart, though. They still managed to make three further sequels and a television series.

Not since some Italian rag had proclaimed loudly 'The Lice of Michelangelo' had Charlton Heston enjoyed such a sensational headline. This time it was an American fan magazine announcing with shocking ferocity '*Charlton Heston – the NUDE love scene that went too far!*' Not the fellow who painted the Sistine Chapel, begged the magazine in earnest. Not the president of the Screen Actors Guild. Not Charlton Heston!

It must have been Kirk Douglas, they suggested. Nope, they
responded to their own shocking revelation. It was Chuck
Heston all right. Wow, what a sensation!

The scene was for a film about an ageing footballer, *Number
One*, in which Heston shares a bed with actress Jessica Walter.
It was all perfectly respectable really; she played his wife. Obviously, someone in the publicity department, deciding that
nobody was likely to find a film about American football as
sensational as one in which Heston has a bed scene, showered
the most daring of the photographs of Heston and Miss
Walter on to the desks of the popular press, and then invited
them to meet the stars down at the studio.

Heston dutifully complied, agreeing to talk about his nude
scene. To the disappointment of the journalists, he said,
'These weren't really nude scenes. We were covered. Here,
I'll show you.' He produced a photograph of himself and Jessica lying in a passionate embrace. 'See, not so much as a bare
breast. These are extremely sensuous scenes, but the expression on Jessica's face, not nudity, gives the effect.'

That point made clear, the fan magazines still intended to
make a meal of the fact that the rumour had spread through
the studio like wildfire that Charlton Heston had bared all.
They certainly didn't seem interested in letting their readership know what it was that had really persuaded Chuck to do
*Number One*.

It had happened in 1963 when Heston read an article about
the life of a quarterback. A motion picture began to form in
his mind. With interest and support from Walter Seltzer, he
approached Dick Zanuck who agreed to pay for a treatment
to be written. Charlton and Walter were delighted since, with
*The War Lord*, they had poured their own money into getting
a script written. But when Dick's father, Darryl F. Zanuck,
still active at Fox, saw the treatment, he turned it down flat.
Eventually United Artists took up the project, promising
Heston a percentage of the profits but with no up-front fee.
So if the picture failed, he stood to make nothing at all. It was
towards the end of 1968 that filming finally began with Tom
Gries directing.

To prepare himself for the role of the quarterback, Heston
spent weeks training with USC's backfield coach Craig Fertic

and the line coach Marv Goux. In the process he put his back
out, suffered agonizing leg cramps, pulled a rib muscle and,
during actual shooting, cracked a rib when a 270–pound footballer charged into him. As he lay writhing in agony, the
footballer had leaned over and said, 'Welcome to the National
Football League!' Swimming in medication and with his ribs
tightly bound, Heston was on the set the following day to
film a football match.

But nobody from the press really cared about any of that,
and, finally, neither did the cinema-going public. The picture
flunked in America, and was hardly seen elsewhere in the
world. And the love scene? It was cut out!

# 22

# Friends, Romans, Countrymen!

CHRISTMAS OF 1967 HAD BEEN SPENT, AS HAD SO MANY OTHERS,
at the lodge in St Helen. During one cold night, Charlton
was awakened by a cable from Peter Snell, a young, almost
unknown producer, proposing that they work together on a
Shakespearean play for television. A series of letters began to
whizz back and forth between Heston and Snell. Charlton
wanted to do *Julius Caesar*, and recognizing that it was his
name that Snell needed to set up any deal, he made his position clear regarding complete script control, casting approval and the role of Mark Antony for himself.

When Snell interested Commonwealth United in his plan,
they decided that such a property and major star as Heston
would be wasted on television, so they began serious preparations to make it into a theatrical motion picture. It would
not, they felt, be the usual classical Shakespeare, but a commercial spectacle with Mr Epic himself, Charlton Heston.
Heston had originally agreed to do the TV film for a fee of

$100,000 plus 15 per cent of the world gross. He was so keen to do the play, and play Antony, that he readily agreed to make the film version on the same terms.

With Heston's name as something of a guarantee, Snell found himself gathering a notable cast: Robert Vaughn for Casca, Sir John Gielgud as Caesar, Richard Johnson as Cassius, Richard Chamberlain as Octavius, Jill Bennett as Calpurnia, Diana Rigg as Portia, and Orson Welles as Brutus. Every name had to be approved by Charlton. But he was not at all happy about the choice of director, Stuart Burge. Snell had to convince Heston, reminding him of Burge's film of Olivier's *Othello*. Charlton was unimpressed. *Othello* had simply been a filmed stage play. But such was his regard already for Snell that he capitulated, maintaining his own specified control over production.

Welles then mysteriously disappeared, so Snell offered Brutus to Jason Robards Jnr, then making *Tora! Tora! Tora!* He accepted and found himself playing a role that he just wasn't cut out for.

During rehearsals Gielgud, certainly one of England's greatest actors, had trouble remembering to leave out the lines that had been cut. He knew the whole thing by heart, and continually flowed into the complete text. Heston gently said to Burge, 'I think John should get his lines back!' He did.

Charlton later found himself back in Madrid, where the locations and particularly the battles for *Julius Caesar* were to be shot. For the first few hours of shooting on the first day, Charlton wasn't needed so he promptly went to sleep on a rock while Robards did the suicide scene. But by the time it came for him to be in shot, he was up and ready. It was early evening, yet still Heston was fresh and full of ideas on how to improve on concepts. He called Burge and Robert Furnival, who adapted the screenplay, and suggested that their last line intended for Lucilius – 'How died he, Strato?' – be given to Antony. He convinced them that that line coupled with the final speech of Antony would bring a new feeling to the close of the play. The three men agreed to the change, and that's how they shot it.

The next day's schedule called for battle scenes involving 600 extras, but the weather report caused them to reschedule.

A day or so later the sun broke through, and Heston, on horseback, followed by hundreds of extras on foot, took up position on a petrified mountain under the direction of second unit director Joe Canutt. These scenes were shot silent, and as Antony's ambush party charge forward, Canutt's voice rang out to cue the waiting extras, 'Acción, caballería! *Acción!*' Each time the cavalry charged, the waiting extras portraying soldiers caught in the ambush, broke ranks and fled. They had been recruited from the local villages and despite the script telling them to stand and hold, they had no intention of being mown down by charging Roman cavalry.

It was while they were on location, that the idea came to Chuck to do something he had always dreamed of.

He says:

I remember a day in Spain when I was riding to the location with Richard Johnson and Richard Chamberlain, and we were discussing Shakespeare. I told them I thought *Antony and Cleopatra* was ideal for a film, and that Shakespeare had even written his play with fifty scenes just like a film script.

I started describing some of these scenes in film terms, scenes I'd been playing in my head for twenty years, ever since I was first in the play as a kid on Broadway. Well, I don't know if I succeeded in convincing them, but I certainly convinced myself.

That afternoon I discussed the idea with Peter Snell and we decided to try it.

Meanwhile, though, they still had to finish *Julius Caesar* at Elstree Studios where the Roman Forum had been recreated for the famous funeral orations. Heston had meticulously worked out exactly how Antony's speech should go. He had been through it with Burge and Furnival, using them as the mob.

'Friends!' he cried. Laughter rose from the crowd. 'Romans!' The mob lost interest. Heston lunged forward, grabbing a passing extra. '*Countrymen*, lend me your ears.' That was the way Heston wanted it done, and that's how he did it. Not that he over-rode the director at all, but he wasn't completely happy with Burge. When they were later shooting the last part of the speech, Heston reached his final lines, 'When comes such another?' The crowd roared.

'Cut!' cried Burge sitting up by his high-angled camera. He looked down at Heston, silent and unsure of what he wanted, but knowing the scene wasn't right. 'Did I do something wrong?' asked Chuck plaintively. Burge sat there, just looking at Heston. The silence was becoming just a little uncomfortable. 'Did I come down the steps too fast?' asked Chuck, begging for a response. 'Well, it would help if you came down a little slower,' Burge replied.

They did another take, and Heston retired to his chair, confident that it had gone well. There was a sudden call back on to the set. They ran through it again, but Burge cried 'Cut' before they were even half-way through.

'Chuck, move over a little bit,' he cried. 'Now, everybody crowd in on him. Move up a step. Now when Chuck mentions the will, I want you all to become a really dangerous, menacing crowd.' Burge had figured out what had bothered him. It had been the crowd, not Heston. But Charlton had been pleased with his own performance, and it niggled him that his director had failed to communicate his dissatisfaction.

It was while he was making *Julius Caesar* that one journalist asked him, 'Would you ever want to direct and produce films?' He replied, 'No. Definitely not. I can function perfectly without directing in terms of casting, scripting and design and so on.' He was certainly able to function creatively in more than just an acting role. He had authority and he also had more muscle than either the producer or the director. When he heard they were considering renaming the film *The Assassination of Julius Caesar*, he retorted, 'I agreed to do Shakespeare's *Julius Caesar*, and that's what it will remain.'

As production neared its end, Heston and Snell began working on plans to make *Antony and Cleopatra*, almost as a sequel to *Caesar*, with Chamberlain reprising his role of Octavius. But the big job was still to get *Caesar* edited. When he got home, Charlton sent a detailed letter to Burge outlining shot for shot the way he wanted his oration scene to be edited, including details of dubbing of the crowd.

When Heston saw the finished film, he was dissatisfied. He had hoped that the play would stand up on its own, but in his opinion the performance of Robards and the film's direction were two hulking great flaws, and he was determined that his own production of *Antony and Cleopatra* would be overseen by the best Shakespearean director available, and that limited the choice to basically two men – Orson Welles and Laurence Olivier.

# 23

# No Longer Just an Actor

THE HAWAIIAN ISLAND OF KAUAI COULD HAVE BEEN THE perfect paradise on which Charlton could spend his time fashioning Shakespeare's *Antony and Cleopatra* into a screenplay. And indeed that's how he spent much of his free time while looking out across the lavender foam on the sand and the dropping sun sparkling on the sea. But somehow he seemed to resent his time beng taken up with filming *The Hawaiians*, a film he simply lacked heart for, but one which he hoped would earn some much needed cash to pour into his own dream.

There was an ironic touch that he should be here making this film which was a sequel to *Hawaii*. After all, he had turned down the part Richard Harris played in the first film, and now here he was playing Harris's son who has become master of the islands. Tom Gries was again his director, but the flair he had displayed on *Will Penny* had waned.

It was a relief to finish the film and get down to the more satisfying, though in many ways more frustrating job of getting *Antony* on to the screen. He began considering numerous actresses for the role of Cleopatra, including Anne Bancroft, Glenda Jackson and Irene Papas, but he could button none of them down. Various potential backers, including a number of major studios, expressed interest in the venture, though towards the end of 1969 it began to look as though nobody would give him the money he needed. As his frustrations increased, so too did the terrible migraines that Lydia was now suffering.

He approached both Olivier and Welles about directing, but neither man could – or would – be the first to direct *Antony and Cleopatra* for the screen. It was another blow to Charlton. When he admitted to Welles that he'd not yet found anyone to play Cleopatra, Welles told him, 'If you don't find a great Cleopatra, you can't do this play, dear boy.' It was the best advice he could have been given.

He was also coming to the conclusion that if he was to get the film made on his terms at all, he might as well direct it himself. Peter Snell told me:

Chuck directed *Antony and Cleopatra* because he could not find a director who was available. He said, 'Oh God, I know the play so well, I'll have a go at directing it with the right cameraman.'

And he did a very creditable job of directing that picture. Unlike most guys who have directed themselves and probably haven't succeeded, Heston never wanted to be a director. But he just found himself in a position where the only way he was going to get that film made was to direct himself.

Chuck finally got around to testing actresses. The two he felt most impressed with that were available were Hildegard Neil and Barbara Jefford. He came to London specifically to shoot tests of them both.

Hildegard recalls her experience of testing for Cleopatra:

Chuck told me he had been looking for a Cleo for a long time. He had been in preparation for about a year and had obviously thought about lots of people, but at the time we met (in the winter of 1970) he was still very much in the searching stage. I was playing Helen of Troy at the Aldwych Theatre, and I believe Chuck saw one of my performances. He must have scribbled my name on a piece of paper.

Some months later my agent rang me up and said, 'We're going to meet Charlton Heston at the Dorchester on Sunday.' He said it was about Cleo. I proceeded to regard the whole thing as rather a far-fetched idea. But I togged myself up because I thought it would be very interesting to meet him.

He met me at the door – a big, wide, generous man. We got on very well, and talked for over two hours. I expected to be there for about ten minutes.

He then saw one of my television plays, *The Casual Affair*, and he arranged to come back in a month's time and do a two-day test. I regarded this as an end in itself, that I was going to have the privilege of playing this lovely part or at least part of it, with Charlton Heston as Antony.

The day after completing his test with Barbara Jefford, Chuck took Hildegard to lunch at the Dorchester. She made some mention about the way her mouth twisted in close-ups, and he looked at her and said, 'You mustn't talk that way about *my* Cleopatra.'

With his test on film available to show to studios, Charlton had to get back to the more routine work of being an actor again.

It was a strange way to begin a film; early Sunday morning in the deserted streets of Los Angeles while Heston walked alone, feeling as if he was the last man on earth. Which was exactly the way he was supposed to feel.

He was making *The Omega Man* – *omega* signifying *the end* in Greek – in which he is literally the last normal human being on the face of the earth, everyone else having become a creature of the night (something like a zombie, or ghoul). Based upon a book called *I Am Legend* which he first first read when making *Touch of Evil*, it's a horror-science-fiction thriller that Charlton had always wanted to make and, even while much of his attention was on setting up *Antony and Cleopatra*, he was also very active in getting *The Omega Man* into production.

He says:

Orson Welles loaned me a copy of it, and I was fascinated. But we were making another picture at the time, and then became involved in other projects. Then, several years ago when I was making a picture with Walter Seltzer, we got to casting around for other ideas. I remembered the book Welles had given me. I knew I had it at home somewhere but couldn't find it.

I told Walter I was sure the title was *My Name is Legion*. Walter was in London then, so he said he'd get it from Foyle's bookshop, and we could talk about it later. When I got to London a few days later, I asked him if he'd read it.

He eyed me suspiciously and asked, 'Are you sure this is the book?'

*My Name is Legion* turned out to be a very thick and weighty tome of population statistics!

Eventually the right book, *I Am Legend*, was located, and Charlton and Seltzer took it to Warner Brothers who agreed to back it. It was directed by Boris Sagal, a rather volatile character, and when there was trouble between Sagal and the cinematographer Russell Metty, Heston was involved in calming things down.

For him, there was no longer such a thing as being a 'routine actor'.

It was the idea of being the last man on earth that appealed to Heston.

Imagine being able to go shopping in a fully stocked store and just pick out what you want. And never have to do your laundry because when a shirt is soiled, you just get a new one.

To have not only all the forty-year-old Scotches and hundred-year-old brandies to stock your bar, but also the treasures of the art museums to hang on your walls.

To film the deserted street scenes we shot on Sunday in the downtown Los Angeles financial district, which is pretty deserted anyway early in the morning. Of course, we needed police to close off a street for three or four blocks.

Part of it takes place on a deserted freeway. For that we used a new freeway that hadn't opened yet. You put some empty cars on it with their doors swinging open and it's a very eerie effect.

He believes there is a moral to the film, similar to the one in *Planet of the Apes*. 'I suppose it's that man is a dangerous animal – possibly the *most* dangerous of all,' he says.

The film was a hit, and coming pretty close on the heels of *Planet of the Apes* and *Beneath the Planet of the Apes*, he was suddenly considered something of a cult figure among the sci-fi buffs. But it wasn't too long before he was back in costume once more – and delighted to be so.

# 24

# The Most Creatively Important Project

HE'D HAD HIS DAILY RUN AROUND LONDON'S HYDE PARK AND was back in his suite on the sixth floor of the Dorchester Hotel. He was in London to prepare his cast for the weeks ahead in Spain when they would re-enact the drama of Mark Antony and Cleopatra. That morning he rehearsed alone, tense but with quiet concentration. Occasionally he interrupted himself, as a director interrupts an actor, and he'd go scurrying to his bedroom to check out something in the reference books. That afternoon he travelled up to Nottingham as the guest speaker for a John Player Lecture at the film theatre. One of the most common questions he was asked that day was 'Why are you wearing a suit embroidered with emus?' He patiently answers each time, 'I accquired this while playing tennis in New Zealand.'

For a man beset by anxieties and expectations about the film he was soon to make, he was remarkably calm. On the way up to Nottingham, one of the car's tyres burst on the motorway. With cool aplomb, he recommended that the other passengers brace themselves just in case the car overturned. As the driver brought the car to a halt, right side up, he calmly pointed out the beautiful view either side of the motorway.

Arriving just a few minutes late for an on-stage interview and facing a full house, Charlton Heston was equally calm in responding to questions. He'd learnt how to deal with these open forums from an audience, and he knew that the same questions were going to come up that he'd answered a million times before. So he knew his answers, just as though he'd read a script for sessions such as this. So when someone asked, 'How did you part the Red Sea?' he answered slowly and deliberately, 'I had a big stick!'

Maybe the audience, like so many others at such lectures or in TV studios, believed they were seeing the man as he is. But it is a performance, his natural shy nature masked by the mass of answers that are in his head. He simply responds to each question with the appropriate answer, and if a new question comes up, then he's quick to create a new answer which he'll mentally file away for future use.

The John Player Lecture was a pleasant diversion from the things that occupied his mind, but when it was over, he allowed his thoughts to be dominated by *Antony and Cleopatra* again, because that was the real reason for being in England.

The cast he had chosen was largely made up of English actors such as Eric Porter, John Castle and Julian Glover. There were also a number of Spanish actors as well as technicians – it was a compromise he'd come to in order to get partial backing from a Spanish movie company. Other money had come from banks, the return of which he had personally guaranteed. He'd thought about that over and over; about whether or not he had the right to spend the money he'd earned for his family's security on something that he just had to do to satisfy no one but himself. He'd discussed it with Lydia, and she supported him wholeheartedly.

He'd remembered the advice both Olivier and Welles had given him; 'You must rehearse the whole play for as many weeks as you can before you start shooting, and you must have a good actor to play Antony for you while you're directing the rehearsals and setting up the shots.'

For three weeks Heston and his cast ran through the play a

dozen times or more shaping it and reshaping it. Recalls Hildegard Neil, also in the cast:

> Chuck wanted to see what sort of directions in which to go. He didn't necessarily want to get everything right in rehearsals, but by the time we had finished two weeks, you had a pretty clear idea of what he was going to be looking for. You were able to go on working with his ideas in your head. It was necessary for him to do this, because when you get to making the film, you become concerned with the position of the camera, where you're going to track to and so on.

The rehearsals, which took place at a dingy hall near Covent Garden, proved he'd been given excellent advice. Just as valuable was the advice that he get another actor to play his part while he directed. He chose Julian Glover who was to play Proculeius which, ironically, was the part Charlton had played on Broadway.

Says Hildegard of Glover, 'He learnt the entire part of Antony and he *played* the scenes with me, which was invaluable. He kept coming up with ideas which couldn't benefit him, but could Chuck and me.'

Heston's praise for Glover is glowing:

> Julian Glover's performance as Proculeius is remarkable, but his equally fine work as Antony through endless rehearsals while I was shaping first the role and then the film is evidence not only of his talent, but his professional discipline.
>
> For an actor to be denied the final act of performance is to take the lady to the ball, wine her and dine her, and then leave her in another man's arms. That he endured this frustration with unvarying good humour is an act of grace for which I can never adequately thank him.

In the summer of 1971 Heston was in Spain with his small army of actors and technicians, transforming it into Rome and Egypt and turning back the time two thousand years. He had just eight weeks to do it all in. The pace was pushed, more compromises than he'd have liked were made, there were

shots sacrificed to save time. But every actor worked his heart
out to give Heston what he wanted. Said Hildegard Neil:

> He worked his guts out. You have such loyalty to Chuck
> because he's enthusiastic, because it means so much to him.
> You also have some awe for this superstar of movies who
> does so much good for the profession, a man who keeps
> going back to the stage because he loves to act on a stage, a
> man who cares so much.
>
> Everyone pulled together and this resulted in a marvel-
> lous atmosphere.

There has probably never been a director who commanded
more loyalty from his actors than did Heston. But what was
more remarkable was that as well as proving to be a competent film director, he still managed to make this Antony one
of his finest performances. But then, perhaps for him to do
this with Antony shouldn't have been too surprising. As he
told me:

> Antony in *Julius Caesar*, which I've played in college, in the
> Bradley film and in the Burge film, has to be the closest to
> being actor-proof of all the great classic roles. If any part is
> a dead cinch, Antony is. It's not only the shortest part of the
> principals but by far and away the best. I mean, poor
> Brutus is hacking away there, you know, getting into all
> this difficult stuff, and Antony wanders on from time to
> time, and has just smashing stuff to do.
>
> Antony in *Antony and Cleopatra* is a much harder role,
> much more difficult than in *Caesar*. But it's interesting to
> have the chance to, in a sense, play the development of the
> man, from the kind of sanguine high drama of *Caesar* in
> which Antony is a triumphant figure, to the growing
> tragedy of the other play in which I think Antony is an ex-
> quisitely written part.
>
> The play itself has never really been successful on the
> stage, and in my opinion the reason for that is that all the
> other great plays take place primarily in the soul of the
> characters – what happens inside Hamlet is far more im-
> portant than where it happens. The fact that Macbeth kills

Duncan in Scotland is not that significant. The fact that Othello lives in Venice is not very important. But *Antony and Cleopatra* is very much involved with the difference between Egypt and Rome. It very specifically takes place in Alexandria, Greece, Sicily and Rome. Also, it's the only one of the great plays in which battles are fought in which the outcome is very significant to the leading characters, and to suggest the Battle of Actium on a stage is almost impossible. It just can't be done, and there are two major battles in it.

This is the one play which really requires a camera. William Shakespeare was a born screenwriter.

As filming progressed, nothing could deter Heston from aiming for his goal. Even when he was taken ill one day, he staggered on to the set, and kept up the pace even in a sickened daze. His own strict code of professionalism led to inevitable moments of anguish. Rafael Pacheco, the cinematographer, seemed to take for ever to light his sets costing valuable time and forcing Charlton to eliminate planned coverage. Other setbacks caused him to consider later that the co-production deal was a mistake. And there were other problems which he had to deal with.

Lydia's continuing migraines were more excruciating than ever, and he wondered just how much he had to do with them. He was also aware that, as he watched the dailies, Hildegard Neil, as fine an actress as she is, was not the great Cleopatra he had hoped for and which Orson Welles had told him he must have. Nevertheless, he reasoned that the play was the thing and that it could still come close to his dream. He knew that as a film-maker, his dream could never be fully realized on any project. But he just wanted to come close. And he tried so hard.

Then, when the eight weeks were over, he stood on the empty monument set, watching them tear it down. He was tired. He'd run the gauntlet and survived, but he was as tired as he could ever remember being. And he looked forward to going home.

But even sheer exhaustion wasn't enough to leach all the pleasure out of making *Antony and Cleopatra*, even with the prospect of all the editing and dubbing that still lay ahead. He told me, 'I liked making that film. It was the most important . . . most creatively important project in my entire life.'

# Part Four

## 25

# A Hero's Welcome

THE LONDON SNOW WAS NOT THE CRISP, TINGLING welcoming stuff that fell on St Helen. As it swirled about outside the entrance to the Queen's Theatre in the heart of London, it was wet, penetrating and miserable, but it couldn't dampen the excitement of the seasoned Fleet Street press who pushed forward to welcome the man emerging from the car like some conquering hero. Charlton Heston had come to town, creating no small stir in the process.

Not that being in London, Charlton's favourite European capital, was anything new, but this time – February 1985 – he had come to fulfil the dream of a lifetime; to act upon the London stage. He had been a professional actor for some forty years; had won a Best Actor Oscar; had received another special Oscar; had made so much money that he never needed to work again – but he had not achieved what he considered to be the pinnacle of any actor's career. He explained, 'I think for every actor who acts in English on the stage, if you don't act in England itself, then you haven't done it yet.' After four decades, he was at last to do it. Really do it. He had come with a largely all-American cast and Herman Wouk's brilliant play, *The Caine Mutiny Court-Martial* which he would both direct and star in as Captain Queeg.

At the press reception at the Queen's, he found himself surrounded on all sides by journalists and photographers. This, of course, was nothing new to him. He knew how to handle these situations. But this time his excitement and enthusiasm

161

for his reason for being in England made this all the more easy and enjoyable as he expounded on his reasons for wanting to act in England, for doing this particular play, for directing it, for his choice of English actor Ben Cross, the star of *Chariots of Fire.*

As Charlton explained, 'With this play you get two charioteers called Ben for the price of one – Ben-Hur and Ben Cross!'

Even before *The Caine Mutiny Court-Martial* was seen by the British public, Charlton Heston was evident in the media, appearing in just about every television chat show, doing radio interviews and doing a few individual press interviews, such was the demand for this now almost legendary movie star to speak to the British public. It had certainly been a long time since Heston had caused such a stirring of interest in London. Age had not diminished his stature or his image – he was sixty-two but still, as one newspaper described him, 'Hollywood's beefiest of sons.'

Yet the success of the play depended on more than just his star image. And he depended on the success of the play. It was by far his most personal and important project since the filming of *Antony and Cleopatra* fourteen years earlier.

Time had healed the wounds which he had suffered through that picture. And if he really believed in what Gordon of Khartoum had said – that his only fear was of failure – then he was all the more determined that *The Caine Mutiny Court-Martial* should not suffer the same fate that his beloved *Antony and Cleopatra* had met with more than a decade earlier.

# 26

# The Trauma of Antony

THROUGHOUT THE MAKING OF *ANTONY AND CLEOPATRA*, Lydia had been savaged by the migraines that were becoming ever more frequent. Why this was so was not evident, but both she and Charlton reasoned that the pressure of making the film that summer must have caused more anxiety than usual for them both.

Certainly Lydia had experienced some worrying times during those eight weeks in Spain. She said, 'On *Antony and Cleopatra* he was so very busy with the directing and acting as well. Usually, he's very careful, and he's an expert swordsman, but I noticed when he came back after one of the battle scenes his hands were all cut about. Of course I worry when he's doing something dangerous, and of course accidents do happen, but you don't think about that.'

Hoping that the headaches would subside once they were back at their canyon, Charlton looked forward to getting home and working on the editing in his own projection room with Eric Boyd-Perkins. But the headaches continued, and Charlton's own frustrations increased as days passed by while he waited for the reels of exposed film to arrive.

Finally they arrived and for more than a month Heston and Boyd-Perkins were locked away editing the 'takes' into a complete film. And still Lydia's migraines continued. It became a race against time as Charlton worked frantically to get the film dubbed and scored on time before the London opening where *Antony and Cleopatra* would get its world *première* in March, 1972. But he found he had to leave the finishing work to Peter Snell, having a commitment to fulfil to MGM to star in their picture *Skyjacked*. He also had to bring his reign as president of the SAG to a close, so pressed was he for time. No sooner had he sorted that out, though, than he found himself elected chairman of the American Film Institute.

163

CHARLTON HESTON

To play the pilot in *Skyjacked*, he did his best to look convincing on film by practising in a jet simulator. In fact, the film called for him to do little else but look as though he could fly a plane. It was hardly the most demanding role he'd ever had in terms of performance. He said, 'Each day I slid into a pilot's belt and flew nowhere on Stage 30. If I was lucky, director John Guillermin let me take ten for a brisk walk to the bathroom before he called lunch. Otherwise I was strapped right there in the cockpit. The only muscles I could exercise there were my vocal chords!'

Somehow the Australian censors felt the film would encourage hijacking, so they banned it. When news of the controversy reached Chuck, he said, 'I cannot conceive of it being controversial for anybody but hijackers, a distinct minority in our society. Nobody is going to argue responsibly that hijacking is a good thing. Our highjacker comes to a richly deserved, abrupt unsympathetic end. This film will not ever encourage anyone to hijack a plane.'

Despite its ban in Australia, the film was highly successful and, even though Heston actually appears in relatively few scenes, he reaped the financial rewards, which was helpful after pouring so much of his own money into *Antony*.

With *Skyjacked* in the can, Heston flew to London for the world *première* of *Antony and Cleopatra* at the Astoria on 2 March. He began that day with an early-morning three-mile run around Hyde Park. Later in the morning he put in a personal appearance at Selfridges in Oxford Street and was mobbed by thousands of fans.

The *première* itself was threatened by a plague of power cuts that were then sweeping the country. A stand-by generator was on hand, but fortunately that night there were no cuts, and Heston's first directorial effort was spread across the Astoria's giant Cinerama screen. But the critics were unimpressed. Said the *Daily Express*, 'The tragedy and the passion ... disappear before your very eyes ... The blame for this unfortunate interpretation must fall squarely on the broad shoulders of Charlton Heston.'

Other newspapers were in general agreement, although the *Guardian* conceded, 'Heston the actor is a different matter.

Here is a solid, four-square and totally adequate performance as Antony.'

Heston was thunderstruck by the reviews, and it is something of a mystery why the critics were so cutting. The film's only real flaw is Hildegard Neil, and it proved Orson Welles's point that the play could never succeed without a great Cleopatra. But apart from that the film is beautifully photographed, evenly paced and generally well acted by almost all the cast. And Heston was superb as Antony.

After its West End showing, *Antony and Cleopatra* disappeared from release. In America it only got shown at one small art house, and that was in a shortened version. Filled with gloom, Heston went to Norway to make *Call of the Wild* and found that he and British director Ken Annakin had fallen in with a bunch of amateurs. The real star of the film was a dog, but the producers of varying nationalities hadn't even acquired the services of a fully trained dog, which naturally held up progress. Finally they found an excellent dog, but *Call of the Wild* became the bane of Heston's life. Ask him about the film, as I once heard someone do, and he'll reply most likely as he did then:

I wish you wouldn't bring up that picture. That was absolutely the worst picture I ever made. I can't even begin to apologize for the script, because if you can't make a good picture out of one of Jack London's greatest novels, you've really screwed things up.

But when I spoke to him about it, I had to admit that I really didn't find it such a bad film. That softened his own comments. He said:

I was disappointed in it because obviously the Jack London novel was just a marvellous story. We should have shot it in Alaska, in the Klondike, and I felt there was a great deal more we could have done with it. More time should have been spent working with the dogs. The film was made under great pressure of time. It was, if you can believe it, a joint Norwegian-German-Italian-Spanish-British co-production, and of course that means you have to have nationals of each of those countries playing a role which meant in turn that I was about the only actor in the picture that wasn't revoiced. And that leads to some complications.

Certainly much of the film worked very well, but I had hoped it might be better.

I've always gotten along with dogs. I've had Shepherds most of my life, and I liked the dog very much. He was a fine dog. He stayed with me a good part of the time in the hotel in Oslo. But I found Norway a somewhat dreary country.

Coming on the heels of *Antony*, all this could well have proven to be a bitter blow for him. But he's never been the kind of actor to just sit and wait for the scripts to come pouring in. He is nearly always instrumental in the setting up of pictures, and for some time he'd been trying to get a film made out of a book he'd read back in 1968 called *Make Room, Make Room*. Eventually MGM picked it up as a star vehicle for Heston with which to follow the phenomenal success of *Skyjacked*. It was a futuristic story about how increases in population and limited food reserves cause chaos. Synthetic food is produced, and one such substance is discovered by a policeman, played by Heston, to be made from dead people. Its name is Soylent Green, and in due course, *Soylent Green* became the title of the film. It certainly looked like the kind of film that could help make the trauma of the *Antony and Cleopatra* failure fade.

# 27
# Husband and Father

CHARLTON AND LYDIA WERE A RARITY IN HOLLYWOOD. IN
March 1972 they celebrated their twenty-eighth wedding
anniversary. The fact that their marriage had survived that
long was almost a mystery. It's a point which Charlton himself deflects with good humour. 'You have to have a certain
amount of mutual tolerance and a basic commitment to the
idea of marriage,' he explains. Then he adds, 'What is really
essential is you must be a superb husband. And I happen to be
a superb husand!'

But, as they have said, their marriage hasn't exactly been
one long honeymoon, and certainly in those early Seventies
the Hestons were riding out a crisis that put more pressure on
their relationship than anything else had ever done, and that
was Lydia's migraines. It seemed that they were caught up in
a horrendous cycle. The migraines caused tension in the
home which caused an added strain on all which only added
to the tension that only increased the migraines. Things came
to a frighteningly critical point when Lydia and Chuck had a
tremendous row. To cool off, Charlton went jogging. But
the situation was not eased. Lydia announced she was going
to Honolulu to write a play.

'Well, do you want me to come along?' asked Charlton.

'No,' she replied.

She spent the next few days in Honolulu until, unable to
bear it any longer, Charlton, Holly and Fray all went out
there to be with her. She and Chuck made up and they stayed
at the lush Royal Hawaiian Hotel for a few days.

For a while the crisis was over, but still the migraines continued and still the pressure was there. Only a year later they
seemed on the point of breaking up again, but at the last
minute they seemed to come to the inevitable conclusion that
they really couldn't live without each other.

167

As well as being a critical time for the Heston family, it was also in many ways a growing one. Fray was now a tall, lean teenager, and Holly was a bright eleven-year-old on the verge of young womanhood. She was also something of a practical joker. Charlton has a favourite story about her:

> When she was eight years old she once successfully got my autograph in a line of kids without my knowing it. And that delighted her beyond belief. There was this whole crowd of kids and I was working my way through them, you know, and Holly came and handed me this thing to sign. Then, later in the car, she showed it to me with great glee.

Fray, now seventeen, was becoming very much an outdoors boy, just as his father had been. That had much to do with Chuck, who made sure that Fray could ride a horse from about the age of eight. He'd also take him off into the desert and teach him to shoot, and on future occasions they both went boar hunting with Joe Canutt. Charlton also encouraged his son to play tennis, but it was the outdoors life that really captivated Fray. In his search for adventure, he became very independent. He told me:

> When I was seventeen I had a truck, and I used to take that truck all over North America. I'd go to Alaska and Idaho for the weekend, and Mexico for a Friday night. I just drove that truck everywhere. I thoroughly enjoyed myself and did it all on a shoestring in those days. I sure had a good time of it, and I think I learned a lot about the country too.

As to why he managed to stay close to his father without ever going through the usual difficult adolescent period, he said:

> That has more to do with my father than with me. He was a strict father, but not a stern one. He was always loving, and my mother as well has to bear some of the credit for the good relationship we still enjoy, because she's always treated me with respect and love and admiration, and I gave

them the same thing they gave me. It's a very easy give and take situation.

When I have children of my own I think I may send them to my parents until they become grown-ups and get them back! I'm sure they could do a much better job of it than I could.

Charlton dotes on his daughter and the fact that she was adopted makes no difference to either him or Lydia. To him she is his 'munchkin', and as he did his best to bring Fray up to enjoy a man's life, so he's gone out of his way to ensure that Holly grows into a perfect young lady. Lydia, however, thinks that sometimes he's gone a bit too far. She says:

You know, Chuck taught Fraser to play tennis so that he'd never be short of someone to play with. But he thought Holly shouldn't learn. I said, 'That's ridiculous. Of course she should learn.' So she did. But he doesn't let me play. You know why? He's the international president of the Society for the Prevention of Women Tennis Players!

One thing that really delighted Charlton about his children is that they never ever showed any signs of wanting to act for a living. He knew from personal and painful experience that it could be a torturous way to earn a living, and whenever he is called upon to go and speak to student bodies about the art of acting, he always does his best to dissuade any of them from setting their sights on an acting career.

Judging by the success he's had as an actor, this may be hard to understand. But Holly even at an early age understood her father's feelings. As she once said to a journalist who couldn't understand why she didn't want to grow up and become a famous movie star, 'My daddy knows lots of actors who are out of work.'

# 28

# 'I'd Rather Play a Senator Than Be One!'

IT WAS HIS BIRTHDAY; HIS FORTY-NINTH BIRTHDAY. FOR A while all those on the set of *Soylent Green* at MGM studios stopped work while a great iced cake was pushed in. It was decorated with a picture of Heston as Moses, made with icing, holding the tablets of the ten commandments.

Everyone, including the director Richard Fleischer, sang 'Happy Birthday!' Only a couple of weeks before Fleischer's famous father, Max, the only producer of animated films to ever seriously rival Disney, had died and work had shut down for a day. But now the mood was of good humour and frivolity, even as the work commenced again, although Dick Fleischer didn't allow the general happy atmosphere to get in the way of the serious business – making what Heston hoped would turn out to be another innovational futuristic thriller.

For the first time since *The Ten Commandments* Charlton was making a film with Edward G. Robinson, now a frail and, although others didn't know it, a dying seventy-nine-year-old. He, however, knew he was dying of cancer, and yet he never missed a day's shooting. Ironically, and as Charlton would find in retrospect, sadly, the last scene Robinson did was his death sequence in which he is gently put to sleep voluntarily while watching films of how beautiful the world used to be. He knew, though still never let on, that this was the last work he would ever do as an actor.

*Soylent Green* was an effective and frightening film, and like the *Apes* sagas and *The Omega Man*, was an immediate hit. He was ready to flex his stage muscles again in actor's country.

He stood in the wings of the Ahmanson Theater in Los Angeles, one of the most prestigious of all American theaters.
Broadway was no longer the be-all and end-all of American
theatre. But just to be in a theatre again, no matter where it
was, after six long years away from the stage, was the elation
that Chuck needed and had missed. There was still that touch
of stage fright, that moment of tension mixed with excitement that came just before going on. And he knew he would
be good in this, *The Crucible*, and he also knew that as a contemporary play, this was second only to *A Man For All
Seasons*. They even played on Christmas night, such was the
success of the play which was completely sold out for almost
every night throughout its five-week run. Ending it triumphantly two weeks into 1973, he prepared himself to recite some
words of Thomas Jefferson.

The recital was for the inauguration of President Richard
Nixon in Washington. He'd supported Nixon, which was
odd simply because he had always voted Democrat before.
But this time he felt compelled to go with the Republicans,
and has remained Republican ever since. Because of his support and his talent, he found himself taking part in a concert at
the Kennedy Center, reading Jefferson to music he really
wished wasn't there.

Before long Heston was back in Washington again, this
time representing the American Film Institute, and while he
was there he got to play tennis with Senator Edward Kennedy
in a doubles game. Charlton and his partner, Senator
Tunney, were wiped out by Kennedy and his partner. But the
real important chore was to arrange for the opening of the
American Film Institute theatre in Washington and also to
strengthen the AFI's position.

There was also an AFI Life Achievement Award dinner for
John Ford back in Los Angeles which Charlton helped to or-
ganize and host. It was attended by President Nixon who also
honoured Ford with the Medal of Freedom. Charlton felt
very proud as chairman of the AFI to have the privilege of in-
troducing the President of the United States that evening.

With so much work taking up his time, and little of it spent
on acting just at the moment, there were added pressures put
on the family which seemed to manifest themselves through

Lydia's migraines. Finally she had to be hospitalized where doctors discovered an enlarged thyroid gland. Charlton actually had enough time to stay in Los Angeles during the days following her operation to support her through her recovery. He hoped that with this long-overdue operation, the terrible problems Lydia had suffered would be gone.

The day he got her home, he had to leave her again which was not easy because just the fact that he was going caused her terrible distress. But he had another film commitment waiting for him in Spain, portraying Cardinal Richelieu in Richard Lester's *The Three Musketeers.*

Originally Lester had wanted Heston to play Athos in this comic version of the Dumas novel. It was to be filmed in Spain, and because Athos was quite a small role yet needed in many scenes, Chuck wasn't at all keen on spending all summer in Spain with little acting to do. So he suggested that Lester give him more of a cameo part, and Lester came up with Richelieu, which Charlton jumped at especially when Lester told him he need only work for ten days.

Heston loved playing the part, not least because it meant hiding behind yet another beard and even a false nose. He has always enjoyed the challenge of creating other men's faces from his own. He also found Richelieu a fascinating character to play. He said:

> The film was a sardonic interpretation of the period and the characters. In fact all the Musketeers are bumbling idiots and certainly the king is. And that's historically accurate.
>
> Now I said to Richard, 'How much of a comic comment do you want me to make?' and Richard said, 'None at all. You must play Richelieu as though we were doing a biographical film about him. He must be an entirely credible antagonist.'
>
> So I played him straight, and although in Dumas's novel he's one of the great black villains, he was in fact one of the most gifted men in the history of France. He was certainly the only man with any real intelligence or capacity in that film.
>
> There was a line that I ran across in one of the biographies of Richelieu that impressed me so much I got Richard to put it in. Someone says to him, 'It must be dreadful to

have so many enemies,' and Richelieu says, 'I? I have no enemies. France has enemies.'

During filming, Lydia came out to be with him, weak but happy just to be with her husband. When Chuck had finished on the picture they went to Germany for a few weeks' vacation, but while there news came that Lydia's aunt, Belle Clarke, had died, which put unwarranted pressure on an already weakened Lydia. Then, just a few weeks later, Lydia's father died.

They flew out to Two Rivers for the funeral, Lydia in a wheelchair suffering from back trouble. There they were joined by Fray who'd been off on one of his adventures. He had plans for being a marine biologist, and was spending a great deal of time away from home, a fact which Lydia was finding hard to bear. It was much more difficult for her than it was for Charlton to let their boy fly the nest, and she found it equally hard to cope with when Fray, just a week after her father's death, left for San Diego to register at the UCSD to study marine biology.

Charlton was still busy in areas other than acting, and found himself again involved with motion picture politics when he was voted back on to the board of the SAG, this time with Dennis Weaver being elected as president. He had even been tempted once to run for the United States Senate when a group of Democrats promised to support him. But as he has often said, 'Quite frankly, I'd rather play a senator than be one. And I've already been President of the United States when I played Andrew Jackson and Thomas Jefferson!'

With so much coming and going, much of it to Washington, life on his ridge was frustratingly spasmodic. But at least Lydia's migraines were less severe now, and Holly was happily entrenched at Westlake High School and taking ballet lessons. She told him quite firmly that dancing was much harder than acting. 'You only have to remember lines and get on and off horses,' she told him.

Towards Christmas of 1973, Charlton took Lydia to Paris for the world *première* of *The Three Musketeers* and there discovered that Richard Lester had split the film into two pictures, the second being *The Four Musketeers*.

Heading home for Christmas they stopped in London for a couple of days where they went to see a portrait of Richelieu hanging in the National Gallery. Lydia looked at it astutely. 'He was a migraine sufferer,' she said.

Richelieu was the only film acting he did that year, with his time taken up so much with other things, and he was itching to get back in front of a camera. It was a difficult time for the movie business. Few films were being made and the tide was turning against the trend of cinema-going. But Charlton was still in demand, and Universal were putting pressure on him to head an all-star cast in a picture they were promising would be earth shattering . . . almost *literally*.

# 29

# Successful Disasters

HE WAS NO FOOL, AND NO MATTER WHAT UNIVERSAL OR director Mark Robson said, he was not going to film an alternative ending to *Earthquake*. He'd told them that he wanted his character killed off at the end and since they had originally agreed to it, that's the ending he was going to do.

It had been that kind of a film. There had been a few times now when Chuck had worked on a film with a distinct lack of enthusiasm for the part or the subject – *Apes II, The Hawaiians*, and now *Earthquake*. He knew he was doing this one mainly for the money with Universal agreeing to his usual percentage of the gross. And Universal certainly expected to make a mint out of this one.

Disaster films were in vogue. Irvin Allen had begun it all with *The Poseidon Adventure*, although you could even stretch the point a bit and say that the cycle began with *Airport* or even *Skyjacked*. But the premise was certainly much the same with a wide variety of soap-opera characters played by big-name stars, all involved with some form of horrific event. Heston termed these pictures 'multi-jeopardy films'.

*Earthquake* said it all, and for added measure this was in a new process called Sensurround which made the audiences feel as though they were literally caught in an earthquake. The cast boasted Victoria Principal, Lorne Green, Geneviève Bujold, George Kennedy, Richard Roundtree and Ava Gardner. But Heston was the name at the top of the list.

Whenever he made a film he always tried to latch onto something to give the picture some importance, some meaning. To him the story was pretty improbable anyway, which is why he felt he should be killed off at the end to give the picture some credence. But the disaster itself, the earthquake, was something which, in California, was quite conceivable.

Said Charlton, 'I feel that one day the scenes depicted in this film could hit Los Angeles. We haven't had any serious earthquakes in Los Angeles, or California, since the 1933 Long Beach earthquake, or the 1906 San Francisco 'quake. There have been several serious tremors, but nothing to compare with these two.' Apart from that, there was little else Charlton could say about the film, except that he got the ending he wanted, and the film was a world-wide hit.

Even before he'd finished work on it, Universal grabbed him for their *Airport* sequel, *Airport 1975*. He accepted it, reasoning that these were the kinds of films which allowed him to earn the money to do the parts that he wanted to do. So as soon as he finished on *Earthquake* he was flying to Washington to begin the *Airport* sequel, which featured everybody as everything from Helen Reddy as a singing nun to Linda Blair as a sick passenger. Heston was the pilot, and as with *Skyjacked*, he took time out to fly a simulator, this time a 747 simulator. 'I crashed it several times,' he admits.

Much of the credit for the success of this film, as Chuck would readily point out, must go to Joe Canutt for the amazing stunt work. A real Jumbo was used for all the sequences, and Canutt himself did the shots of the Heston character passing from a moving helicopter to the damaged but still airborne Jumbo, although this sequence also utilized miniatures.

The demands on Heston's acting abilities are few in films like *Earthquake* and *Airport 1975*. He explains:

Most of the acting parts are more or less chemical contributions. The audience needs someone they can identify and
say to themselves, 'He's going to do something about all of
this.' And because people know me as an authoritative
presence, there's no problem in featuring me as a person
who takes charge of a holocaust.

Part of the reason for this is my shadow. No matter how
versatile an actor may be or how he strives to widen his
range, he must deal with his shadow. And my shadow has
been Moses, El Cid and Michelangelo, not to mention a
president or two. If you need a chariot race run, a ceiling
painted or the Red Sea parted, you think of me.

So in these films it isn't necessary to explain that my
character will be responsible. You don't have to take time
out to explain that to the audience. It's built in.

He was visibly shaken as Fray spoke to him on the phone, and
as Charlton relayed the news to Fray's mother, Lydia felt desperately helpless for her son, and wished he'd come home.
Fray was ringing to tell them of the terrible events of the previous day. Years later, Fray related that incident to me:

I was working as an apprentice on a raft as a river guide. I
was in the back of the raft with about ten people on board
and the head of the outfit was steering. We hit a freak wave
and the raft flipped. We were all trapped underneath, I
managed to get clear and swam ashore and got help. But a
few people were drowned. It was a very sad, dreadful incident. It does go to show you that the wilderness can be very
dangerous.

It was about that time – although that incident had nothing
to do with this decision – that he decided to switch from
studying marine biology at UCSD and take up literature at
the University of California at Los Angeles. Charlton warned
him that writing for a living was no easier than acting as a
career. But Fray was at that time being drawn into the film
industry and while at UCLA he also studied film, and
through his skill as a writer of both fiction and non-fiction, it

'Why, there then: thus do I escape the sorrow
Of Antony's death.'
Eros (Garrick Hagan) plunges the sword into himself, falling dead at his
leader's feet in this first screen adaptation of *Antony and Cleopatra* (1972).

Heston as lawman Sam Burgade is caught by outlaw Zach Provo (James Coburn) in *The Last Hard Men* (1976). The picture below shows him much more splendidly dressed, but still bearded, as Henry VIII in *The Prince and the Pauper* (1977).

And still bearded: with Brian Keith in *The Mountain Men* (1979), the first film written by Heston's son, Fraser.

In *Mother Lode* (1980) Fraser Heston performed double duty as screenwriter and producer in a modern-day adventure drama directed by and starring his father.

was only a matter of time before he sat down to write a screenplay.

With two 'disaster' movies out of the way, Heston felt it was time to get down to some real acting, and he responded to Robert Fryer's request that he do *Macbeth* at the Ahmanson in the early months of 1975. Fryer suggested that Peter Wood, of the British National Theatre, direct, and so Heston went to London to meet with Wood and his Lady Macbeth, Vanessa Redgrave. Wood and Heston worked together on cutting the play, and Charlton was greatly stimulated by the harmony with which they worked. Vanessa, however, felt that the Bard's words shouldn't be touched at all and Wood, sensing that her main fear was that the superstar of epic movies was changing her role to benefit him, reassured her that this wasn't the case, and she responded warmly. But she still didn't like the idea of the text being changed at all.

Heston's estimation of her as an actress and a pro was high. He told me, 'Politically, Vanessa Redgrave may make Jane Fonda look like Herbert Hoover, but she comes to work on time, and she is a bloody brilliant actress. I have the utmost respect for her as a creative artist and as a professional. Although, of course, I disagree with her politics.' So warm was the relationship between them that she and her lover, Franco Nero, as well as her children, spent Christmas with the Hestons at their Coldwater hideaway.

Despite all expectations, when the play opened the critics were as cruel to this as they had been to Heston's *Antony and Cleopatra*. But that didn't affect the audiences who came enthusiastically, and there were plans in progress to bring it to London for the summer of 1976. That, however, didn't come to pass, which disappointed Charlton who wanted passionately to act upon a London stage.

He couldn't know it then, but his time would come.

Tennis had always been something of an obsession with Charlton. He used to play it just for fun, but as his status as a celebrity grew, so he became more involved in special tournaments. In the spring of 1975, he went to South Africa to take part in a tournament in Johannesburg for the Black Tennis Foundation. He went on to play in numerous pro-celebrity

matches, including the King of the Hill and one to raise money for the Muscular Dystrophy Fund. For such matches he usually partnered Fray's good friend Martin Shafer who, in just a few years' time, would be instrumental in getting Fray's first screenplay filmed.

What Charlton really enjoyed doing was having the real tennis pros over to play on his private court. His boast is, 'I've probably played more great tennis pros than any other lousy player in the world.' The joke among his family is, 'When he dies and knocks on the Pearly Gates, if the devil taps him on the shoulder and says, "How about a game of tennis?" he'll go!'

Tennis was what Charlton did for fun. He's never considered acting fun. That, he says, is hard work. But he was happy to put his tennis talents on display for good causes, and the one in Johannesburg he felt was worth it because it was the first major tennis tournament in that city's history that was totally racially integrated.

What he didn't feel was worth his time and effort, however, was the SAG. The problem was probably more to do with him than the actors' union. He disagreed with many of their policies, and the whole thing was, for him, becoming a waste of his time. So he finally left the board for good and went back to being a piece of chemistry again, this time for *Midway*. This was one of those big epic-sized, all-star-cast war pictures in the tradition of *The Longest Day* and *Tora! Tora! Tora!* But although a war picture, it was really another multi-jeopardy film for Universal. By now they seemed to figure that Charlton Heston was something of a good-luck charm for these big event movies.

Much of the film was shot aboard the *Lexington*, the one remaining US Navy carrier from World War Two, and again the studio used their Sensurround gimmick to simulate the rumble of exploding shells. The picture did great business, and Universal immediately pressed Heston to star in *Two-Minute Warning*. They seemed determined to milk Heston and this genre for all they were worth.

This time, the film was the story of a sniper taking pot shots at a huge football crowd with Heston as the cop trying to get to the sniper before the bullets really start flying. And

when they do, the crowd panics in a terrifying sequence that now seems all the more horrifically real since television showed us the real-life disaster of May 1985 when panic swept through a crowd of football supporters in Brussels' Heysel stadium and 38 people died.

Although Charlton really had very little to do in the film – indeed, he spent whole weeks waiting to be called to the set during production – it was an excellent film, tightly and tautly directed by Larry Peerce. But it was not a commercial hit, which must have staggered Universal as it did Heston. The success of the disaster films had come to an end.

30

# Taking Pains to Stretch

SUCH IS THE STATURE OF HESTON THAT VERY OFTEN HE IS approached by a studio to commit himself to a script even before the director or any other actors have been chosen. These situations give Heston both director and cast approval, and in this way he continues to wield a considerable amount of authority over his films.

Such was the case with *The Last Hard Men* for Twentieth Century-Fox. It was a western about an outlaw out to get the retired marshal who imprisoned him. Heston was set to play the marshal, and he hoped that they might get Sean Connery as his co-star and Jack Smight, who worked with Heston on *Midway* and *Airport 1975*, to direct. Walter Seltzer was putting *The Last Hard Men* together so Charlton tended to go along with his choices which, eventually, were James Coburn to play the outlaw and Andrew V. McLaglen. This was ironic in that several years earlier Heston had turned down *The Way West* mainly because he was not impressed with McLaglen's work on *Shenandoah*, which in itself is odd seeing that *Shenandoah* has to be one of the finest films made about the American Civil War since *The Red Badge of Courage*. Which goes to show that not even Charlton Heston is always a good judge of films.

He actually found McLaglen to be a very competent director, although he was somewhat impatient with Coburn who tended to be more of an introspective actor than Heston. Coburn liked to discuss and argue every point in the script until he felt he could believe it, which wasted some time on the set and this naturally frustrated Heston.

Heston, of course, was not an actor to just sit back when another actor came up with an interpretation of a scene or a line of dialogue different from the director's vision – or the writer's or even Heston's. This has even happened when he and a director have occasionally clashed, only then it's usually the director who gets his way. But when Barbara Hershey, who played Chuck's daughter in *The Last Hard Men*, came up with a different interpretation of how she should react in one scene, Heston sided with McLaglen and for hours there were discussions and arguments before they got the scene in the can.

Very much aware of the authority which Heston exerts on a film set (occasionally to the chagrin of other actors), McLaglen told me:

I really like Heston, both as a person and an actor. He's very hard working. Now I know some people will say he's this or that on the set. Well, I just think that's governed by the parts he's played. I mean, he's certainly been successful in epics like *Ben-Hur* and *The Ten Commandments*. But he's a good man and I like him. I like him as an actor, and he was very nice to work with.

*The Last Hard Men*, only moderately successful, remains one of Heston's most explicitly violent films with plenty of Peckinpah-style blood-letting. In fact, McLaglen told me, it was so gory that when it was censored for showing on American TV, they ended up with such a short vesion that McLaglen and his editor had to go back into the cutting room and put in some of the less bloody out-takes to lengthen it again.

Heston has always boasted that he can sleep anywhere at any time. He has a metabolism that simply shuts down almost at will. This may not be much of a gift to benefit other people, but it certainly helped him to endure the two-hour session he went through each day while being made-up to look like King Henry VIII for his cameo part in *The Prince and the Pauper*.

Not even the make-up for Richelieu took so long, although he could recall spending some two hours or so being made-up for the older Moses so many years ago. He always enjoyed the task of finding the right face for each character but he became easily bored with the daily process of being made-up, so he slept through some of it.

Despite his role as Henry being so brief, he still went to great lengths to find the right look. He says:

> The first thing I go into on any project is the design of the make-up. I wear a great many putty noses, wigs and false beards. My make-up man is Siegfried Geike and I think he's the best in the world. I really begin to get inside a character when I'm at that stage with Ziggy – designing the make-up.
>
> When I played Henry VIII I used something like a modern English accent, but one suspects that Henry didn't talk much like a modern Englishman. But no one is quite certain how he did sound.

He was also delighted to have the chance to film on location, under the direction of Richard Fleischer, in England at Penshurst where Henry had actually stayed. Soaking up the historic atmosphere, Charlton was able to relive a few days from the life of the fat old king.

By now Chuck had decided to slow down on the number of films he was making. In recent years he had been filming almost back to back, and when he failed to get the part of *MacArthur* which he had so badly wanted – Gregory Peck played it – he came to the conclusion that he was becoming over-exposed in too many pictures. So the only other film he made in that year, 1976, was *Gray Lady Down*, the story of a submarine stranded at the bottom of the ocean.

To prepare himself he managed to get permission to spend some time on a nuclear submarine while it ran mock torpedo attacks on surface vessels.

The film was directed by David Greene whose rather undistinguished credits included *Godspell* and *Madame Sin*. His main problem had been in choosing, or in being chosen for, less than interesting vehicles, and *Gray Lady Down*, a superior 'event' picture, allowed him freedom to exercise his own style as well as make a commercial picture. He certainly impressed Heston. The latter always made it a policy to stand off-camera so that actors in close-up can talk to him, whereas many other actors allowed their stand-ins to do that kind of job. But when Heston had to talk to an off-camera character, he insisted he could do it without an off-stage actor; Greene noticed this and how it affected his performance.

'Chuck,' he said, 'I know you're only trying to give as efficient a performance as possible, but that doesn't necessarily make what you do creative. Getting it right isn't getting it good. So how about we put a couple of off-stage actors over here and you give your lines to them.'

Heston agreed, and he had to admit after the next couple of takes that Greene was right.

*Gray Lady Down*, released in 1977, did well and gave Charlton the chance to play more of a performance than the earlier Universal disaster epics had done. The canvas here was smaller, but the tension and the drama of the seemingly impossible rescue operation made for the best of Heston's contemporary films of that decade.

Early in 1977 he finally did a play he'd been preparing to do for a year, Eugene O'Neill's *Long Day's Journey into Night*. Charlton considered this rather gloomy nightmare based on O'Neill's own complex relationship with his family, the best American play ever. He'd seen it at its world *première* and just knew that he had to do it. It wasn't a case of wanting others to like him in it. It was simply a play he had to do. And Robert Fryer wanted him to do it at the Ahmanson Theater where he was beginning to feel very much at home.

Fryer managed to acquire the services of Deborah Kerr, but at some cost to Heston. She insisted on first billing. Charlton let her have it. He wanted her as the wife and was prepared to

take second billing. To his delight Bruce Dern took the role
of Jamie who has inherited consumption from his drug-
addicted mother. As the play progresses, the mother sinks
into madness, and the son burns with frustration and hatred
for his family, especially for the tyrannical, miserly, insensi-
tive father, played by Heston.

It was a big challenge for Heston. 'It's really something
daunting for me,' he said. 'I think an actor has to take pains to
stretch a bit. If you only do parts you're absolutely positive
you can bring off, your range keeps contracting all the time
until finally you're only doing one part, and I think that's a
grave mistake.'

By this time he had also stretched himself in other areas,
promoting the cause of acting. He was co-chairman of the
Center Theater Group, which included the Ahmanson Theater, and he was still chairman of the AFI (American Film Institute) and a member of the National Council of the Arts.

He also, that year, went on to win The King of the Hill
tennis tournament with his partner Martin Shafer, but he
slowed down on his film commitments. Not that he wasn't in
demand any more – offers were pouring in, such as the lead in
*Raise the Titanic* which, like so many others, he turned down.
'I'm one of the lucky seven or eight fellas they can still hang a
movie on,' he said at the time. 'I do the best of what I'm
offered.'

It was in 1976 that I first met Heston, during a whistle-stop
tour to promote *Midway*. In fact, he spent a great deal of time
that year touring the world promoting that picture which
actually became one of the highest grossing films of that year,
beaten at the box-office only by *The Omen* which, ironically,
he had turned down.

As for his home life, things were going much more
smoothly than in recent years. The tremendous pressures
he'd had heaped upon him, or which he'd invited, had taken
their toll on his private life. But he had hung on to what he
had and by the end of 1977 he was a more than contented
man, not least of all because his children had by now proven
that they had no intention of becoming actors. He says:

Thank God, because it's a miserable way to earn a living.

I've done well but they have the perception to realize that my experience is hardly typical. There are about 35,000 members of the Screen Actors' Guild in America, and seventy-five per cent of them make less than the official poverty wage.

Fraser is studying creative writing – also a terrible way to earn a living. Holly, who is now fifteen, is still at school. She doesn't want to go into show business. She's an intelligent girl.

But perhaps what really satisfied Charlton about his home life was that Lydia's migraines had stopped at last. Not long ago one of my colleagues, Ken Ferguson, asked her how she cured the migraines. She told him, 'I just stopped taking all the tablets that were supposed to kill the pain.'

# 31

# From the Wind River Mountains to the Valley of the Kings

'CHARLTON HESTON IS A POMPOUS ASS, AND HE'S LOUSY AS Ben-Hur.' That's what Bette Davis has gone on record as saying, although she's also said a lot worse about other stars. But in 1978 at the fiftieth Annual Academy Awards ceremony it was Bette Davis who presented Charlton with the Jean Hersholt Humanitarian Award in recognition of his contributions to community and film work. Miss Davis noted how he had visited troops in Vietnam twice, made overseas tours for the State Department's Cultural Presentation Program, had worked on the President's Council on Youth Opportunities, as well as served six terms as president of the SAG.

As he waved his Oscar in the air, she hung on to his arm and gazed adoringly into his eyes. He could have had no idea just how scathing her impressions were of him. But Heston is thick-skinned enough not to let things like that bother him. It's his thick skin, he says, which helps him to shrug off the lousy reviews the critics have sometimes bestowed upon him.

However, Miss Davis is not the first person to describe Heston as 'pompous'. Perhaps he is, but it has, I feel, more to do with masking his shyness than anything else. As he has said, his observation of himself is as 'dull and square'. He doesn't make headlines, and so he is very much a respected figure in the world of movies. And I have been told by one publicity officer how, during a drive out to Heathrow Airport, he never spoke a word. Yet that is the natural Heston, shy of strangers, unable to put on a performance every time just for the benefit of others.

He is also a man of numerous skills. He is an avid sketch artist, and spends much of his spare time on film sets taking impressions of his fellow-artists and the crewmen. Some years ago he even had a series of his drawings on display in galleries in New York, London and Glasgow.

He is also – though he hates doing it – an accomplished writer. In 1978 he allowed his personal journals which he had kept since 1956, to be edited and published, revealing not just the inner feelings of a generally unknown personality, but also a flair for using words. The journals, published as *The Actor's Life*, provided an insight into the day-to-day proceedings of film-making as well as his private life, though many of his more intimate moments, such as his parents' divorce, were not included. It was a fascinating study of how one man saw himself, his life and his work. But it covered a mere twenty years of his life.

I suspect that the publication of his journals was actually a ploy to fend off publishers urging him to write his autobiography – which will almost certainly never be written. He was once asked to write one thousand words for the record sleeve for the soundtrack of *Antony and Cleopatra*. He managed after two weeks to get as far as 750 words. He never finished the task and the record sleeve was printed minus Heston's notes.

'You'd scarcely credit the thousand ingenious excuses I found to put it off,' he said. 'I'd rather play the first act of *Macbeth* than write a thousand words.'

His journals became quite famous for some of the rather unflattering remarks he had to make about some of his leading ladies. 'That,' he told me, 'was because they were never written for anyone else but me to read.'


It was while Heston was in London promoting *The Actor's Life* that he told me he was going to make a film called *Wind River* which his son had written. He told me proudly, 'Happily he wrote it and sold it before he came to me about it.'

It's not too surprising that eventually Fray should choose to look to the cinema as a means to express himself as a writer, and later as a producer. Although Charlton had done his best, and successfully so, to dissuade Fray from becoming an actor, he nevertheless allowed him to work on some of his films. For instance, on *Antony and Cleopatra* Fray was the second assistant to Joe Canutt. Naturally, his interest in movies was deep-rooted.

Fray told me how he came to write *Wind River*, which was later changed and released as *The Mountain Men*:

> I had not consciously avoided going into the film industry, but I did not seek it. I had other interests and I still have a passionate interest in marine biology and oceanology. But I found myself in the film industry some years ago when two associates of mine, Martin Shafer and Andrew Scheinman, came to me and read an outline for a novel I'd written called *Wind River*. And they said, 'You know, we think you should write a screenplay and we could make a movie out of it.' And that's what we did.

With the help of Martin Ransohoff, they interested Columbia before the film was offered to Heston senior. Charlton recalls:

> I knew he was writing a script. He didn't try to conceal it but he didn't try to get me to read it either. He just didn't

show it to me and I've never asked to read anything that he didn't ask me to read. You never ask a writer if you can read something. If they want you to read it, they'll ask you to read it.

The part is so clearly right for me that I suppose he actually wrote it for me. Ethically it was quite correct for him not to suggest the script to me and to keep me apart from it till he sold it, and I understand that and admire him for it.

Later, I knew they'd sold the script and that the studio wanted to show it to me. I must say that when I did read it, I opened it with some trepidation. I thought, 'What if I hate it?' And I confess that I thought to myself that if it is at all possible to do, then surely I must do it for Fraser, to get him started. But it's an incredible part for me.

It's set in the Titons, the Wind River Mountains, and is about the fur trade that flourished there for a very short time; just a generation. These trappers – Free Trappers, they were called – enjoyed the greatest freedom of probably any group of people at any time. But this freedom was bought at great cost. They lived very hard and dangerous lives, constantly threatened by the elements, dangerous animals and hostile Indians.

It's the story of two such men, played by myself and Brian Keith, and it covers their lives over a course of a year as the fur trade was coming to an end. It's really a story of freedom.

And the rarest thing he's got in, which is something that is seldom in parts that are tailored for me, is a great deal of humour.

It's by far the best part I've had since *Khartoum*.

*The Mountain Men* was filmed in Wyoming and directed by a first-time film director, Richard Lang, son of Fritz Lang. Charlton was fifty-six, but still fit and strong, which he needed to be for this extremely physical film. He said:

I was doing a scene with Steven Macht, who plays my enemy, Heavy Eagle, for the climax of the film. It was a ferocious, savage battle and we were both covered in blood and just *exhausted*. We'd been shooting since seven that morning and it was now evening, and we were determined to finish the sequence.

It was gone seven, and the sun was low, and I was lying on my back in the dust. Steven was leaning on me with blood running down his chest and dripping on to me. And I suddenly looked up at him and said, 'You know, Steve, when we were kids and playing cowboys and Indians, our mothers would have called us in to supper by now!'

He adds wryly, 'I mean, it is a ridiculous way to make a living!'

Fray was constantly on the set, working in close association with Richard Lang. Charlton seemed aware that his son watched over the proceedings with a director's eye:

It's a curious thing, but he does have that attitude. He's very keen but nevertheless very green. He has a remarkable successful relationship with Richard Lang who seems to like having Fraser on the set.

He still seems very young to me, although I suppose sons always seem younger to their fathers than they are. But he *is* young at just twenty-four. But he's very cool and easy and has a good quality of captaincy in him. He'd be a good fellow to be with if the house caught fire or the car broke down in the middle of the mountains. That works equally on a movie set too, so that will stand him in good stead one day when he chooses to direct.

I must say, I find in him as a writer qualities that I also find in him as a son. He's honest and diligent and thoughtful and sensitive to the needs of other people. And I respect that in him as a writer and love him for it as a son.

Making the film wasn't all happy families though. Charlton told me:

One of the problems of *The Mountain Men* was that Martin Ransohoff, having promised me he would let Joe Canutt do the action scenes, reneged on those promises and let a first-time director from television direct the action. Lang didn't know how to do it. The only scene that Joe Canutt directed was the scene with the rapids, which was terrifying. And I can boast shamelessly about the action there because I didn't do it. Joe Canutt did. But he should have done all the action scenes leaving Lang to concentrate on the actors. Unfortunately, that didn't happen.

My feeling was that there was too much money spent on the film. It was a very good script, but some of the best things were cut out.

*The Mountain Men* failed to deliver the goods and reach the expectations that both Heston senior and junior had hoped for.

'Every film-maker has his ruined baby,' says Charlton. '*The Mountain Men* was mine.'

Charlton Heston strode about the Egyptian tomb, his famous but travel-weary knees on show beneath khakis. Behind him walked Susannah York, her huge eyes bulging at the sight of ancient relics lost for centuries until now. Heston's voice was filled with awe as he spoke of this great find, the tomb of an Egyptian princess.

Only this wasn't Egypt. It was Lee International Studios in London, and Heston and Susannah York were filming a scene from *The Awakening*. I was watching from the sidelines. Someone told me that the technical advisor on the picture, a little man who kept popping up, could actually read the hieroglyphics that covered the fake tomb walls spread across the sound stage.

Charlton finished his scene and walked over to me. This was the third time I'd met him. I'd previously met him when he was in London promoting *The Actor's Life*, and before that during his *Midway* tour. He was much more at ease with me than before as he led me to his dressing-room. This was a more relaxed Heston than I'd met previously. Before, I had been one of a succession of journalists ushered in for a thirty-minute interview. And on those occasions, his weariness at having to answer a couple of hundred questions – many of them repeated – in one day showed.

But this time he was full of enthusiasm for the work he was about and eager to talk about it:

I play an English archaeologist and the part calls for me to
age from 43 to 61. I guess I'm getting a minor reputation as
the only American actor they'll allow to play Englishmen!
And I must say I'm delighted because it allows me the
chance at parts I wouldn't otherwise be offered. And it's
also an interesting role in that there's a time span of eighteen years, which is a very hard span to reach for an actor.
For a thirty or forty year span you just put on rubber and a
white beard and wig and you're home and free. But eighteen years is kind of tricky.

I'm in the young part this morning. It consists largely of
putting very nice make-up around my eyes and darkening
up the grey in the temples. For the older part we've deep-
ened all the lines which are certainly already there but need
to be deeper. And we've darkened the sockets of the eyes
and put much more grey in the hair. I also put on a beard
for that which is partly grey. And it seems to work.

It was difficult though to come here because I had just
finished *The Mountain Men* – we talked a bit about that
when we last met – and just six days after I was standing
chest deep in a beaver pond in filthy buckskins and a red
beard and long red hair playing an 1830s American mountain man, I found myself in an academic gown at London
University lecturing on archaeology. That was a *long*
jump, much longer than the distance from the great Titon
Mountains in Wyoming to London. The interior journey
was the longer one. But I've gotten comfortable with it
now.

They engaged a very good – actually he's Welsh – actor–
director called Hugh Thomas to work on my English
accent with me.

Even while I was filming in Wyoming my wife, Lydia,
said, 'Shouldn't you start working on your English
accent?' I'd have come apart in the middle if I'd have come
home in rancid buckskins, put my feet up and started
working on my English accent with a tape recorder. I had a
different kind of accent for *The Mountain Men* and trying
out another would have ruined both movies.

When Heston is relaxed like this, it isn't difficult to get some good long answers – even statements – from him. He told me how much he was impressed with Mike Newell, the film's director, especially since it was his first motion picture. Knowing just how much authority he carries on and off the set, I asked Heston if he looked for direction, especially from such a new name as Mike Newell. He said:

Oh, you must look for direction. Even on the stage which is actor's country. Even on stage you must have some shape given. I've never heard an actor say he didn't like to be directed. If they ever said it, they're out of their bloody minds. You can't do it by yourself.

Acting is all smoke anyway, of course. It's the least significant of the arts because it has no material existence. You can't pick up a can of film even and say, oh yes, how marvellous. You have to run it when it can only exist in time. There's nothing there to touch. With a book or a play or a statue, there is something there. You can make changes to it. You can't do that with performance. And there's nothing to be sure of and you therefore are just trying . . . it's all in the dark. It's like trying to assemble something with your eyes closed. It's all hit and miss really, and you can't examine it too closely anyway or it won't work. So for all these reasons you desperately need someone looking at it and saying this part was good, that part wasn't, couldn't we do this. Because you have to feel you can try anything you want, and let someone else shape it and squeeze it in at the end and so forth.

Whenever I play someone, it doesn't matter who it is or whether he actually lived or not, I like to find the outside of the man first; what he looks like, what he wears, what he sounds like, the way he walks. I can't find the middle of the man before I find the outside. Other actors I've heard say 'I must start in the centre' which sounds plausible. But it helps me to find my way into a character if I can latch on to something, like the kind of khakis he wears, the kind of boots. These boots in fact are very old. They're my shooting boots. They're at least eighteen years old, and I wear them because they're very comfortable and when we get to

Egypt, we'll be climbing around the rocks, and I chose
them also because they're right. I looked at a lot of pictures
of archaeologists and studied what they wore. When I decided that these were the right boots, that gave me something to go on, and I'll wear the same boots for the later
scenes when he goes back to the desert as the older man, but
then I won't wear shorts because he's supposed to be sixty-one.

The film itself was a development in the tradition of those
old mummy pictures. The princess that they discover is rein-
carnated as Heston's daughter, played by Stephanie Zimbalist, real-life daughter of Efrem Zimbalist Junior and star of
TV's *Remington Steele*.

The whole cast and crew evidently held Heston in high
esteem, and young Stephanie was positively in awe of him.

I enjoy working with Heston. He's going to be excellent in
this film. I remember when I was twelve, I saw *Ben-Hur*.
It's one of the two best movies I've ever seen, and I just had
this big crush on Charlton Heston.

He's playing for character in this, not like the usual leading man roles. He's very bold, he's not afraid to be too big,
and I admire that. He's also a nice guy. Not every good
actor is necessarily a nice guy.

I'm learning a lot from him just by observing him. Like
listening to the questions he asks which wouldn't have
occurred to me, like where is the bottom of the frame
because he has a flashlight in the scene and if it's below the
frame nobody'll see it. Just little things like that which
never would have occurred to me. Of course, he's been at
this a lot longer than I have.

I paid another visit to the studio a week later and found
Heston playing the older part. All the make-up he spoke
about was there and he had a sort of an older stoop, giving
him something of a tired look and very effective. He told me
that he's made so much money from his earlier films that he
could retire now if he wanted to.

'Then why don't you?' I asked.

'Because acting is my life,' he replied.

He also told me how much he was looking forward to going back to Egypt. 'I haven't been there since we made *Khartoum*,' he said, 'and I do look forward to it. It's a remarkable country, and with this story you couldn't do the scenes without being there.'

For about a month *The Awakening* crew worked on location, some of it spent in the world-famous Egyptian Museum in Cairo, but most of it in the blistering heat of the Valley of the Kings. To give me an idea of how hot it got, Chuck much later told me, 'The temperature did get up to 130 degrees Fahrenheit, and if you have to pick up a metal prong and you must cool it by pouring water on it before you do the shot, you could say it's *warm!*'

# 32

# The Best Set of Electric Trains

HE WAS FIFTY-SIX, YET HE STILL RAN FOR AN HOUR EVERY morning, still played tennis and still went after the best parts the theatre could offer. In 1979 he was back in the robes of Sir Thomas More again for another resounding success in Robert Bolt's *A Man For All Seasons*, and he was better than ever in the part. For him, coming back to plays like this and *Macbeth* was progression. He *had* to improve his performance each time he did them, and because these were roles he had played so often before, he could measure his growth as an actor against these portrayals. He was still looking to become the actor that he still believes he has not yet become. For him, he must stretch himself to the limits, though what those limits are he doesn't yet know simply because he's not been there yet. He figures that if and when he does, that's the time to call it a day. But being the perfectionist he has always been, he will never be satisfied, and he knows it.

In 1980 he continued to expand himself ever further, this time playing a role that had been done a million times before – Sherlock Holmes. The play at the Ahmanson was *Crucifer of Blood*. Its success led to what Heston deems a fairly radical offer. He said:

They wanted me to do *Crucifer of Blood* on television. I liked the part, but it wasn't the kind of thing that would do as a film – at least, I didn't think so. So when the TV offer came up, I asked, 'How many days?' They said, 'Twenty-one.' 'Only twenty-one?' I said. The shortest picture I ever made in my life was *Touch of Evil* with Orson Welles who is a pretty clever fellow, and that took thirty-nine days. I told them I just couldn't do my best work in twenty-one days – not as good as I could, say, in forty-six days.

Besides, in America, not so much in Britain, there's this perception that audiences will not go to see actors in theatrical films whom they can see on their TV screens in a series. In a sense this seems ridiculous. One of my movies must be on TV somewhere, every night of the week.

I still make a living doing films and I'm in that happy group of guys who have control about *who* you work with, *how* you do it, and so on. I don't really want to mess that up, even to play Sherlock Holmes.

All his working life Charlton had resisted temptations from television networks to appear in TV films or series. Often it's been to the point of virtual seduction. As far back as 1957 MCA were dangling a carrot worth a million dollars in front of young Heston to do a western series, *Cimarron*. But he resisted. He has avoided tele-film like the plague, displaying a somewhat snobbish attitude towards it, believing that because of the speed with which television series and films are made, he could never produce the kind of performance that would satisfy him, let alone anybody else. He had, of course, been happy to do television when it went out live because then it provided similar challenges to a stage performance. But since *Elizabeth and Essex*, he hadn't worked at all in TV, except as a celebrity guest in chat shows and even entertainment shows. Basically, his premise was, if you can do film for cinema, don't do TV.

Under Ronald Reagan, Charlton had first become involved in motion picture politics when he was invited to join the board of the Screen Actors Guild. That, in turn, led to Charlton being elected six years in succession as president of the SAG, following in Reagan's footsteps. But Heston has no intentions of following the path Reagan took to the White House in 1981. Because of his involvement in film politics, the question of whether or not he ever intends to run for senator or even president of the United States is often put to him, and, as we've seen, his stock answer is, 'I've already been president of the United States twice.'

Even as recently as 1984 there were rumours flying that he intended to run as senator for the Republican Party in California, but again he quashed these reports with the familiar 'I'd rather play a senator than be one.'

It's certainly true that he maintains a strong interest in politics, and he's thrilled to see his close friend Ronald Reagan presiding over America. Shortly after taking office, President Reagan appointed Heston as Chairman for the Arts on the Presidential Task Force on the Arts and Humanities.

His involvement with presidents didn't finish there that year. Almost immediately after the killing of President Sadat, he received two offers on the same morning to play Sadat in planned movies that never materialized. But such is the authority that the Heston image carries that when any film-maker wants to find someone to portray a president, they invariably turn to him.

By the end of 1981 he was back on a film set, but this time he was playing a dual role as well as directing again. The picture was *Mother Lode*, and it was thanks to Fraser that Charlton came to make his best film since *Planet of the Apes*. Fray told me:

I spent a great deal of time in British Columbia and the Yukon in Alaska, and it occurred to me that the tales of Jack London were every bit as contemporary in our times as they were in his. I thought, why not do a modern day

adventure but with planes instead of dog sledges, and do a
suspense adventure drama story in modern times about the
search for the mother lode?

Fray's excursions into the rocky wastelands came during
the making of *The Mountain Men*. Accompanied by a former
hard rock miner, he was given access to gold and silver
mines, and learned of the feuds, suspicions and eccentricities
of hardened old prospectors. There were stories of miners
who concealed their discoveries from others and even murdered their partners. Some miners went mad in the process.

Fray's screenplay told of two young adventurers who go
looking for the mother lode, only to meet up with a grizzled
old prospecting Scotsman and his demented twin brother. It
had elements of real horror and suspense, and he decided to
produce it himself. Naturally he showed his script to his dad
who loved the idea of playing twin brothers, and they
brought Peter Snell on to the scene to act as executive producer to give support to Fray in setting up the production.
Their next task was to find a director. Fray says:

I suggested to my father that he direct it because I felt he
could do a better job than anybody else, and I was right. He
knew the script almost as well as I did, and he knows that
country and he knows those kinds of men.

He didn't take it lightly or ill-advisedly. He considered it
quite carefully for a long time. I made no attempt to persuade
him. I made my case that he was the best man for the job.

Heston senior told me:

When I directed *Antony and Cleopatra* it kinda leached the
creative pleasure out of acting and directing. I found that
the pressures of directing one of Shakespeare's major
tragedies and acting one of his major roles at the same time
was pretty overwhelming. I determined then that I would
never direct another picture that had a part with that kind
of heavy responsibility that Antony had.

I've had one or two offers to direct since and I've
responded in more or less those terms. For instance, if

there's no part at all in it for me, I don't want to do it. And if it's a huge part it really would be too tough for me to do, although other actors do it like Clint Eastwood.

After I accepted the roles in *Mother Lode*, it was Fraser who first suggested to his associates and then to me that I direct it.

He said, 'You know, this is really what you've been talking about all along. You're only in about half of this script.'

And I hadn't really counted the pages, and then I thought, 'That's true.'

Also, since the parts I play in this are two Scottish brothers – and I don't do accents readily, unlike Peter Ustinov – I had to work quite a long time on the accent, and thus spent many months working on the parts as an actor. So a lot of my normal preparation work as an actor was behind me, and I thought, 'This is the one to do.'

Assembling a small cast of Nick Mancuso, John Marley, Dale Wilson and Kim Basinger before she became a major star, Heston moved his unit off to Canada to film in Vancouver's damp forests. Heavy, unremitting rain failed to halt filming which was almost simultaneously done by two units, the first under the direction of Charlton Heston and the second under Joe Canutt. Heston knew from his experiences on *El Cid, The Mountain Men* and a number of other films the importance of giving the second unit director full control of his unit. He told me:

Joe Canutt is a secret weapon. Some of the best work in *Mother Lode* unquestionably was shot by Joe Canutt. He is the best action director in the world. It is to Steven Spielberg's disadvantage that he doesn't realize that. Spielberg is a marvellous director, but directing action is not the best thing he does. Action directors do that better.

As a matter of fact, I shouldn't be telling you this because this is a secret I want to keep. But John Ford, Willy Wyler, George Stevens and Cecil B. De Mille used second unit directors all the time.

But I would also want it known because I'd like to see Joe prosper, yet there's still a part of me that would like to keep this as a secret that only I know, and that is for a director to have good action scenes like we had in *Mother Lode*, you have to have somebody who knows how to do it. So I'm delighted you asked me about it, because I don't know how the current trend of gifted directors can fail to take this lesson from the generation that preceded it.

As far as directing is concerned, he said:

Directing films is, as Orson Welles once said, the best set of electric trains any little boy ever had to play with. But it's very hard work. A simple way to do it is that a good director never sits down on the set. Even if you can sit down, you shouldn't because it slackens the tension.

The analogy I frequently draw upon which is dead accurate is that making a film, particularly on location, is like a military operation. The total reliance on the weather, communications, transportation, food, morale, alternate options – leadership is exactly the same in both situations.

We had difficulties with the weather. British Columbia is notorious for its unreliable weather. We were working in mountains and rainy forests. When we were shooting in a mountain lake – which we reached by twenty-three miles of winding road which was gradually being washed away each day by rain – and I had five days of shooting up there, each day as I drove up there and back I felt exactly like a platoon commander in the infantry. And I often thought, 'What if I'm cut off here and the battalion goes on down the pass?'

Never before had Charlton and his son worked in such close collaboration. As director, Chuck conferred constantly with Fray as screenwriter and producer. On past films such as *Major Dundee* and *Touch of Evil* conflict had arisen between directors and producers or studios. With Heston senior as both star and director and Heston junior as producer and screenwriter, it seemed that confrontations could come in any shape, whether it be between producer and director, or director and writer. But, as Fray was quick to point out, this was not the case.

In my experience, the conflict has been between the writer and the producer, which to me was interesting because I had to resolve that within myself. That's almost more difficult than resolving the one between the producer and director, and in this case the director was my father who's very easy to get along with. In making this film I learned a lot from him, and I think we learned a lot about each other. We rarely had conflicts that are confrontational by nature. We've certainly had disagreements. In that respect it makes for more fun because you have to resolve these things to the advantage of the film and not your own ego. You have to take your ego and throw it away. And fortunately I feel I can take the example of my father who is very good at putting his own interests aside and setting his sights on what is important to a scene or even a single shot. He knows what every shot is there for. If it doesn't have a reason for being in the film, he won't show it.

They finished the film in spring 1982, when the whole Heston family came to London where *Mother Lode* was to be scored. A press conference was arranged for their arrival which was where I got to meet them all and discover just how differently Heston performs for a crowd of journalists as opposed to one. He seemed to thoroughly enjoy himself, moving from one group of interviewers to another. As time wore on, Fray came over to him while he was expounding on the pros and cons of Vanessa Redgrave.

'Come on dad, we've got to get going,' said Fray.

'Not now,' beamed Charlton. 'I'm telling one of my best stories on Vanessa Redgrave.'

But Fray could see that his dad was tired, as I had noticed too. He was looking decidedly older at fifty-eight and he seemed to have lost that princely walk. I think, however, he was more tired than old.

'Okay dad, but don't be too long,' said Fray.

So Heston continued to hold court, his voice higher and jollier and much more flippant than in the private interviews I'd held with him. The group of journalists, myself included, responded heartily to his stories, and it all the more encouraged him to continue. He performed magnificently, just for us.

The fact that his family, with the exception of Holly, was there was more to do with work than a family vacation. Apart from the fact that father and son were making the picture together, Lydia had served as stills photographer, and Fray's wife, Marilyn, whom he had married two years previously, had served as assistant to the producer as well as unit publicist.

Her comment on her father-in-law was, 'As a director, he was inventive, even-tempered, humorous, thoughtful, somewhat impatient of unnecessary delays and thoroughly familiar with every word in the screenplay. His voice was seldom raised.' Which is pretty much what she thinks of him away from the film set too.

When asked about his family, Charlton says:

You know, people often ask me if it worries me that I don't see enough of my children. But I say, 'On the contrary, I see rather more of my children than most fathers do.' This is certainly true now that I am able to control what I do and when I do it, and often even where I am going to do it. We were all together in the Canadian Rockies for *Mother Lode*. So no, I never worry about not seeing enough of my children.

# 33

# Political Problems

WHEN HE HAS SOMETHING TO SAY, HESTON SAYS IT, USUALLY with great eloquence and tact, but he gets his point across. He doesn't expect everyone to agree with him, especially when it comes to politics. That he should pick up a few enemies along the way, however, is surprising to even contemplate. It's true that on film sets his own high standards have not always met with everyone's approval; those who disapprove are usually they who set their sights a lot lower. Richard Harris, for instance, vowed he'd never work with Heston again.

Undoubtedly, when he's on a film set he makes it clear that he expects people to be on time and to know their lines. He exercises the authority which he's earned on film sets, and most people respect it. But the very idea of Heston making enemies off the set seems contradictory to his nice guy image. But in recent years, because of his political convictions, he has earned for himself enmity from one or two prominent names.

The first is Paul Newman. It all began when they both appeared on an American TV show, debating the case for and against nuclear weapons. Heston made it clear that he felt there should be no freeze on weaponry. Newman disagreed, adamant that there should be one. In the debate Heston proved more solid and articulate and came off better in the heated exchanges. As far as he was concerned, it was over and done with, but Newman was seething, and their falling-out was a public embarrassment. But, for the moment, the matter was dropped and generally forgotten.

Meanwhile, Charlton was under pressure to accept the lead role in a TV mini-series, *Once upon a Murder*. He wasn't convinced he could do it, or even wanted to. 'I took a look at the set-up for a mini-series a few years ago,' he said, 'and discovered they wanted to film fifteen pages a day. At that speed, who can give their best? From the cameraman to the make-up artist, everyone is working against the clock and that rarely makes for a perfect end product.'

But then he heard from Gregory Peck and Richard Chamberlain that a lot less haste went into the making of these television blockbusters these days. Heston checked it out, and when he was told they would film only five pages a day, he accepted it. It was set in the deep South, and he played a banker and founding father of a fictional American town. It was set between the years 1920 and 1960, which appealed to Heston's sense of character.

'One thing I enjoyed was all the make-up creation,' he says. 'I age forty years and end up wearing a white wig above a face full of wrinkles.'

That same year, 1983, he generously gave up all his movie memorabilia, donating it to the Theater Arts library of UCLA. The vast collection included scripts, scrapbooks, letters and speeches. So much of it was there that it had to be stored in a separate room, which was called The Charlton Heston Room.

He was also chosen that year as honorary high chief of New York's first highland games. Since his mother's parents were members of the Fraser clan, he was honoured and proud to be invited, and even turned up in a Fraser kilt. He also willingly obliged with a show of strength by having a go at tossing the caber, but the thing nearly fell on him. 'Compared to that,' he gasped, 'parting the Red Sea was dead easy!'

But life was not all fun and games. Old wounds inflicted upon Paul Newman had not healed, and he'd never forgiven Heston. The whole sorry case was brought to the surface again when Charlton was invited to host a charity event in aid of a fund to help drug addicts. It was the Scott Newman Foundation, named after Paul's son who had died so tragically a drug addict. This, of course, made no difference to Heston, who was glad to give his support in aid of a worthy cause. But when Newman heard that Heston had been invited, he made loud protests and insisted that the invitation be withdrawn. It duly was and Donald Sutherland was invited at the last minute in Heston's place. Charlton was furious, and the rift between the two superstars widened.

The following year Heston's political beliefs, which he stated loud and clear, earned him further enmity, this time from Ed Asner, better known as the star of television's *Lou Grant*. And this time the situation became potentially dangerous. Asner was the president of the Screen Actors Guild and was involved in trying to merge the SAG with the Screen Extras Guild, a move which Charlton objected to and actively opposed. So much so that he co-founded the AWAG—Actors Working for Actors Guild.

During a meeting chaired by Asner, he accused Heston and his supporters of fostering a 'master race mentality among performers'. Heston was enraged, and he demanded an immediate apology from Asner, contending that the 'master race' remark branded himself and the rest of the AWAG as

Nazis. Asner refused to apologize. Not long after that, Heston began receiving anonymous death threats, prompting him to write publicly 'clearly Mr Asner's radical allegiances and El Salvadorian rebel enthusiams trigger the adrenaline in the extreme fringe of his supporters.' The Los Angeles Police, taking the death threats seriously, mounted a more than usually diligent watch on Heston's Coldwater home.

Undeterred by these political problems, Charlton and Fray made plans for a new spectacular epic, *The Overlord*, set at the time of the Trojan wars. Fray wrote the screenplay and plans to direct it. At time of writing it is still in the preparation stages, and it is to be hoped that it doesn't suffer the same fate as another historical epic Charlton hoped to make a few years back called *1066*. That was a subject he had long wanted to do but never found a satisfactory script relating the momentous events in history when England was conquered by the Normans.

In 1980 Peter Snell revealed to me that he had found a script and that Heston was interested and wanted to play William the Conqueror. Snell at that time had also interested George C. Scott in portraying King Harold. 'The only problem,' Snell had told me, 'is getting the money. The film industry doesn't like costume epics. The public likes them, but not the industry.' Heston confirmed his interest to me, but said, 'I'd love to do it, if only he can get the backing.' Snell never did get the finances to produce *1066*. Heston hopes that *The Overlord* won't be another pie-in-sky project, and he's already set Joe Canutt to direct the second unit.

Yet these kinds of problems really paled into total insignificance towards the end of 1984 when the world's attention was captured by the horrendous plight of thousands upon thousands of men, women and children literally starving to death in Ethiopia. Heston made a personal visit to the drought-stricken country with the American Red Cross, to see first hand the harrowing suffering of a whole nation in a desperate effort to promote aid. He visited one of the camps where people were dying in their hundreds, and he noted how pitifully inadequate the medical resources there were.

'There were two doctors,' he said, 'six nurses and thirty-four grave diggers.'

It was an experience that made him aware of how privileged he had been – and still is. He tried never to take for granted the luxuries he enjoys which even to those of more humble means in civilized countries are nothing more than dreams.

But with the status he has gained in the world, as insignificant as it sometimes seems when compared to world happenings, he has tried to use it for what he has believed to be good causes. Celebrity has its influence, sometimes only as far as gaining publicity is concerned, but wisely used, it can get results. And Heston is not a man who's afraid to say what he believes, or do what he feels is right. Quite a contrast to the scared-to-death teenager who lived in Chicago and the loner whose simple backwoods life promised security in solitude.

But even with all that he now had, he'd still not done *it*. He was, however, about to.

# 34

# He Finally Does It!

It was February 1985, when Charlton Heston came to the Queen's Theatre in the heart of London to meet the press and tell them of his new play, *The Caine Mutiny Court-Martial*. He said:

> The West End of London has more of an allure for an American actor than Broadway does for an English actor. I can't imagine English actors finding the same feeling of, I guess, coming home, going back to your roots, when they play on Broadway. But that's what the American cast I brought over here for *The Caine Mutiny* felt when we all stepped on the stage of the Queen's Theatre.

He was to direct the play, as well as star as Captain Queeg.

I've directed both on the stage and in films several times, and *Caine Mutiny* seemed an ideal choice to undertake both roles as actor and director. Queeg's part is divided into two very long scenes of about twenty minutes each. But he isn't on stage the rest of the time, so when he's on stage he's doing most of the talking. The rest of the time I was able to concentrate on directing.

Because of union rules forbidding American actors to dominate the entire casting of a play or show, there have been problems in the past whereby American roles have had to be filled by English actors. The same is true, though vice-versa, in the States. But this time a special deal was worked out. Explains Charlton, 'Robert Fryer and Duncan Weldon negotiated an exchange agreement between British Equity and American Equity which allowed Alan Bates to bring an all-British company to the Ahmanson last year and now we are bringing *Caine Mutiny* with almost all American actors to London.'

Heston is himself critical of the union's stringent rules. He says, 'the unions have had restrictions against the importation of foreign artists. But I've never talked to a working actor in either country that didn't say, "Oh, we don't want to keep that rule; let's just work in either country."'

Curiously enough, Heston didn't choose a Shakespearean play to make his English stage debut. But he explains his reasons for choosing *The Caine Mutiny Court-Martial*:

I wanted to do an American play. I also wanted, for my own reasons, to do a play I hadn't done before. And *The Caine Mutiny Court-Martial*, as events have proven, is an extraordinarily durable piece. The compelling appeal of courtroom drama is hard to explain because by definition, of course, people are talking about events that have happened before the play started, and happened somewhere else, and you never get to see anything. But when they work, they are overwhelming, and the audience response to *Caine Mutiny* is very gratifying.

But it was to be a little while yet before a London audience would respond to *The Caine Mutiny Court-Martial*. It wasn't due to open at the Queen's until April, and before that they were to play the provinces.

Unfortunately, they had picked one of the worst winters of recent years, and the American cast felt the chilling effects. Even Charlton, who'd braved the icy wastes of Norway for *Call of the Wild* and thrilled to the snowfalls in St Helen, had trouble keeping warm, especially when they played Brighton. Slipping out of the chilly hotel where they were staying, Charlton found a seafront chemist. The girls behind the counter could hardly believe their eyes when they saw, beneath a hooded anorak, Charlton Heston enter and ask for a hot water bottle. But the bottle was to little avail. By the time the company had arrived in Birmingham to break all house records with the play, Charlton was suffering from a heavy cold which he fought back with every performance.

Finally they came to London, the spring weather typically wet and cool. It was an emotional moment when Chuck Heston set foot on the Queen's stage to perform. He had finally done it.

The critics even rose to the occasion, giving the play and Heston exhilarating notices. The *Daily Express* said of Heston: '. . . towering central performance of immense heroic stature', and the *Sunday Mirror* described the play as 'powerfully entertaining and thought provoking'.

The audiences flocked to see it, and for three months Heston, Ben Cross and the rest of the company went on to that stage and met with a nightly tidal wave of adulation. It was the highlight of Heston's career which had so far spanned almost forty years.

Elated and flushed with success and the response he met with from the British audiences, he willingly accepted an invitation to put his hands in cement in London's Leicester Square where a 'star pavement' was laid to emulate the world-famous feet and hand imprints outside of Hollywood's Chinese Theater where Heston's feet had some years previous been pressed into wet cement. His hand prints in London were joined by those of Sir John Mills, Dame Anna Neagle, Omar Sharif and Alan Bates.

June came and went all too fast. *The Caine Mutiny Court-Martial* had enjoyed a long, full run. And then it was all over.

On the last night, Heston, as usual, stood in the wings breathing in the final moments of a successful run, trying to savour every precious moment of it. This was actor's country, and as with every final curtain on a winning play, he felt the elation and the tinge of regret that it was over. He went home.

There was still much to do. There was a tennis tournament to play, a new epic film to try to get off the ground, other parts to look for, to keep stretching himself, to try to become the kind of actor he still dreamed of being.

He had even finally allowed himself to be seduced into committing himself to a television series. Aaron Spelling was prepared to pay Heston a record $80,000 an episode to star in the spin-off from *Dynasty—The Colbys*. Spelling's aim with the new super-soap was to wash away all the others, and signing Heston was his first big move. And as back-up, he also signed Barbara Stanwyck as the family matriarch, Constance Colby, whose scheming with Uncle Jason Colby, played by Heston, leads to the break-up of the Carringtons and the Colbys. Consequently, Heston, Stanwyck and their family, including Emma Samms as the new Fallon, head for California, heralding the new series. And, unlike the Carringtons who never seem to go anywhere, the Colbys jet-set it to far-off exotic places such as Monte Carlo and Rome, ensuring that the budget for *The Colbys* exceeds even that of the costly *Dynasty*.

Agreeing to star in a TV series is an unprecedented move on Heston's part, but it can only further enhance his super-star status by exposing him to a whole new generation of fans who probably never got to see the likes of *Ben-Hur* and *The Ten Commandments* on a real, big, silver screen. It can also only make him richer than ever. But what is uppermost in his mind in accepting this assignment is that he wants to keep on acting in parts that will stretch him and still keep him firmly in the public eye. And after so many years, he has conceded that television is now the medium which can best do all those things. But he still probably won't be satisfied.

He remains his most hardened critic. He told me,

I'm satisfied really with my work in none of the films I've made or plays that I've done. I think that's healthy. I've certainly made films and done plays that I like, and on an overall basis I'm content with the total. But I've never seen one of my own film performances with which I'm really content, and I would presume that's healthy.

I guess when I am totally content, it'll be time to hang it up and practise being a mean old man, sitting by the fire and hitting people in the knees with a stick!

# Filmography

**1941**

*Peer Gynt*   Produced and directed by David Bradley from the play by Henrik Ibsen. Cast: Charlton Heston, Kathryne Elfstrom, Betty Hanisee, Roy Eggert Junior, Betty Barton. (Re-released in 1965 with synchronous music by Edvard Grieg.)

**1950**

*Julius Caesar*   An Avon Production presented by Carl J. Ross. Produced and directed by David Bradley from the play by William Shakespeare. Cast: Charlton Heston, David Bradley, Grosvenor Glenn, Harold Tasker, Robert Holt, Theodore Cloak.

*Dark City*   A Paramount Picture. Produced by Hal B. Wallis. Directed by William Dieterle. Screenplay by John Meredyth Lucas and Larry Marcus. Cast: Charlton Heston, Lizabeth Scott, Viveca Lindfors, Dean Jagger, Don DeFore, Jack Webb.

**1952**

*The Greatest Show on Earth*   A Paramount Picture. Produced and directed by Cecil B. De Mille. Screenplay by Fredric M. Frank, Barre Lyndon and Theodore St John. Cast: Betty Hutton, Charlton Heston, Cornel Wilde, Dorothy Lamour, Gloria Grahame, James Stewart, Henry Wilcoxon.

*The Savage*   Paramount. Produced by Mel Epstein. Directed by George Marshall. Screenplay by Sydney Boehm, based on the novel by L. L. Foreman. Cast: Charlton Heston, Susan Morrow, Peter Hanson, Joan Taylor, Richard Rober, Don Porter.

*Ruby Gentry*   20th Century-Fox. Produced by Joseph Bernhard and King Vidor. Directed by King Vidor. Screenplay by Silvia Richards. Cast: Jennifer Jones, Charlton Heston, Karl Malden, Tom Tully, Bernard Phillips.

*The President's Lady* 20th Century-Fox. Produced by Sol. C. Siegel. Directed by Henry Levin. Screenplay by John Patrick, from the novel by Irving Stone. Cast: Susan Hayward, Charlton Heston, John McIntire, Fay Bainter, Whitfield Connor.

*Pony Express* Paramount. Produced by Nat Holt. Directed by Jerry Hopper. Screenplay by Charles Marquis Warren. Cast: Charlton Heston, Rhonda Fleming, Jan Sterling, Forrest Tucker, Richard Shannon.

*Arrowhead* Paramount. Produced by Nat Holt. Directed and written by Charles Marquis Warren, based on the novel by W. R. Burnett. Cast: Charlton Heston, Jack Palance, Katy Jurado, Brian Keith, Mary Sinclair.

*Bad for Each Other* Columbia. Produced by William Fadiman. Directed by Irving Rapper. Screenplay by Irving Wallace and Horace McCoy, based on McCoy's novel. Cast: Charlton Heston, Lizabeth Scott, Dianne Foster, Mildred Dunnock, Arthur Franz, Ray Collins.

*The Naked Jungle* Paramount. Produced by George Pal. Directed by Byron Haskin. Screenplay by Philip Yordan and Ranald Mac-Dougall, from the story *Leiningen Versus the Ants* by Carl Stephenson. Cast: Eleanor Parker, Charlton Heston, William Conrad, Norma Calderon, Douglas Fowley.

**1954**

*Secret of the Incas* Paramount. Produced by Mel Epstein. Directed by Jerry Hopper. Screenplay by Ranald MacDougall and Sydney Boehm. Cast: Charlton Heston, Robert Young, Nicole Maurey, Yma Sumac, Thomas Mitchell, Glenda Farrell.

**1955**

*The Far Horizons* Paramount. Produced by William H. Pine and William C. Thomas. Directed by Rudolph Mate. Screenplay by Winston Miller and Edmund H. North, from the novel *Sacajawea of the Shoshones* by Della Gould Emmons. Cast: Fred MacMurray, Charlton Heston, Donna Reed, Barbara Hale, William Demarest.

*Lucy Gallant*   Paramount. Produced by William H. Pine and William C. Thomas. Directed by Robert Parrish. Screenplay by John Lee Mahin and Winston Miller, from the novel *The Life of Lucy Gallant* by Margaret Cousins. Cast: Jane Wyman, Charlton Heston, Claire Trevor, Thelma Ritter, William Demarest.

*The Private War of Major Benson*   Universal. Produced by Howard Pine. Directed by Jerry Hopper. Screenplay by William Roberts and Richard Alan Simmons. Cast: Charlton Heston, Julie Adams, William Demarest, Tom Considine, Tim Hovey, Sal Mineo.

**1956**

*The Ten Commandments*   Paramount. Produced and directed by Cecil B. De Mille. Screenplay by Aeneas MacKenzie, Jesse L. Lasky Junior, Jack Gariss and Fredric M. Frank. Cast: Charlton Heston, Anne Baxter, Yul Brynner, Yvonne De Carlo, John Derek, Nina Foch, Debra Paget, Judith Anderson, Edward G. Robinson, Sir Cedric Hardwicke, Martha Scott, Vincent Price, Henry Wilcoxon.

*Three Violent People*   Paramount. Produced by Hugh Brown. Directed by Rudolph Mate. Screenplay by James Edward Grant. Cast: Charlton Heston, Anne Baxter, Gilbert Roland, Tom Tryon, Bruce Bennett, Forrest Tucker, Elaine Stritch.

**1958**

*Touch of Evil*   Universal-International. Produced by Albert Zugsmith. Directed and written by Orson Welles. Cast: Charlton Heston, Janet Leigh, Orson Welles, Joseph Calleia, Akim Tamiroff, Marlene Dietrich, Zsa Zsa Gabor, Joseph Cotten.

*The Big Country*   United Artists. Produced by William Wyler and Gregory Peck. Directed by William Wyler. Screenplay by James R. Webb, Sy Bartlett and Robert Wilder from the novel by David Hamilton. Cast: Gregory Peck, Jean Simmons, Carroll Baker, Charlton Heston, Burle Ives, Charles Bickford, Chuck Connors.

*The Buccaneer*   Produced by Henry Wilcoxon for Cecil B. De Mille. Directed by Anthony Quinn. Screenplay by Jesse L. Lasky Junior and Bernice Mosk. Cast: Yul Brynner, Charlton Heston, Claire Bloom, Charles Boyer, Inger Stevens, Henry Hull, E. G. Marshall, Lorne Greene.

**1959**

*Ben-Hur*   Metro-Goldwyn-Mayer. Produced by Sam Zimbalist. Directed by William Wyler. Screenplay by Karl Tunberg (and Christopher Fry – uncredited) from the novel by Lew Wallace. Cast: Charlton Heston, Stephen Boyd, Haya Harareet, Jack Hawkins, Hugh Griffith, Martha Scott, Cathy O'Donnell, Frank Thring.

*The Wreck of the Mary Deare*   MGM. Produced by Julian Blaustein. Directed by Michael Anderson. Screenplay by Eric Ambler from the novel by Hammond Innes. Cast: Gary Cooper, Charlton Heston, Michael Redgrave, Emlyn Williams, Cecil Parker, Alexander Knox, Virginia McKenna, Richard Harris.

**1961**

*El Cid*   Allied Artists-Samuel Bronston-Deare Film (Rome). Produced by Samuel Bronston. Directed by Anthony Mann. Screenplay by Philip Yordan and Fredric M. Frank. Cast: Charlton Heston, Sophia Loren, John Fraser, Raf Vallone, Genevieve Page, Gary Raymond, Herbert Lom, Douglas Wilmer.

**1962**

*The Pigeon that Took Rome*   Paramount. Produced, directed and written by Melville Shavelson, from the novel *The Easter Dinner* by Donald Downes. Cast: Charlton Heston, Elsa Martinelli, Harry Guardino, Brian Donlevy.

*Diamond Head*   Columbia. Produced by Jerry Bresler. Directed by Guy Green. Screenplay by Marguerite Roberts from the novel by Peter Gilman. Cast: Charlton Heston, Yvette Mimieux, George Chakiris, France Nuyen, James Darren.

*55 Days at Peking*   Allied Artists. Produced by Samuel Bronston. Directed by Nicholas Ray. Screenplay by Philip Yordan, Bernard Gordon and Robert Hamer. Cast: Charlton Heston, David Niven, Ava Gardner, Robert Helpmann, Flora Robson, Leo Genn, John Ireland, Paul Lukas, Harry Andrews.

**1965**

*The Greatest Story Ever Told*   United Artists. Produced by George Stevens in creative association with Carl Sandburg. Directed by George Stevens. Screenplay by James Lee Barrett and George Stevens, based on the book by Fulton Oursler and writings by Henry Denker. Cast: Max Von Sydow, Michael Anderson Jr., Carroll

Baker, Ina Balin, Pat Boone, Victor Buono, Richard Conte, Joanna Dunham, Jose Ferrer, Van Heflin, Charlton Heston, Martin Landau, Angela Lansbury, Janet Margolin, David McCallum, Roddy McDowall, Dorothy McGuire, Sal Mineo, Nehemiah Persoff, Donald Pleasence, Sidney Poitier, Claude Rains, Gary Raymond, Telly Savalas, Joseph Schildkraut, Paul Stewart, John Wayne, Shelley Winters, Ed Wynn.

*Major Dundee* Columbia. Produced by Jerry Bresler. Directed by Sam Peckinpah. Screenplay by Julian Fink, Oscar Saul and Sam Peckinpah. Cast: Charlton Heston, Richard Harris, Jim Hutton, James Coburn, Michael Anderson Junior, Senta Berger, Warren Oates, Ben Johnson.

*The Agony and the Ecstasy* 20th Century-Fox. Produced and directed by Carol Reed. Screenplay by Philip Dunne, from the novel by Irving Stone. Cast: Charlton Heston, Rex Harrison, Diane Cilento, Harry Andrews.

*The War Lord* Universal. Produced by Walter Seltzer. Directed by Franklin J. Schaffner. Screenplay by John Collier and Millard Kaufman, from the play *The Lovers* by Leslie Stevens. Cast: Charlton Heston, Richard Boone, Rosemary Forsyth, Maurice Evans, Guy Stockwell, Niall MacGinnis, Henry Wilcoxon.

**1966**

*Khartoum* United Artists. Produced by Julian Blaustein. Directed by Basil Dearden. Screenplay by Robert Ardrey. Cast: Charlton Heston, Laurence Olivier, Richard Johnson, Ralph Richardson, Alexander Knox, Nigel Green, Michael Hordern.

**1967**

*Counterpoint* Universal. Produced by Dick Berg. Directed by Ralph Nelson. Screenplay by James Lee and Joel Oliansky, from the novel *The General* by Alan Sillitoe. Cast: Charlton Heston, Maximilian Schell, Kathryn Hays, Anton Diffring.

*Will Penny* Paramount. Produced by Fred Engel and Walter Seltzer. Directed and written by Tom Gries. Cast: Charlton Heston, Joan Hackett, Donald Pleasence, Lee Majors, Bruce Dern, Ben Johnson, Slim Pickens, Lydia Clarke (Mrs Heston).

**1968**

*Planet of the Apes* 20th Century-Fox. Produced by Arthur P. Jacobs. Directed by Franklin J. Schaffner. Screenplay by Michael Wilson and Rod Sterling, from the novel *Monkey Planet* by Pierre Boulle. Cast: Charlton Heston, Roddy McDowall, Kim Hunter, Maurice Evans, James Whitmore, Linda Harrison.

*Number One* (also known as *Pro*) United Artists. Produced by Walter Seltzer. Directed by Tom Gries. Screenplay by David Moessinger. Cast: Charlton Heston, Jessica Walter, Bruce Dern, John Randolph, Diane Muldaur, Mike Henry.

**1969**

*Beneath the Planet of the Apes* 20th Century-Fox. Produced by Arthur P. Jacobs. Directed by Ted Post. Screenplay by Paul Dehn and Mort Abrahams. Cast: James Franciscus, Charlton Heston, Kim Hunter, Maurice Evans, Linda Harrison.

**1970**

*The Hawaiians* (GB title *Master of the Islands*) United Artists. Produced by Walter Mirisch. Directed by Tom Gries. Screenplay by James R. Webb, based on the novel *Hawaii* by James A. Michener. Cast: Charlton Heston, Tina Chen, Geraldine Chaplin, John Phillip Law, Alec McCowen.

*Julius Caesar* Commonwealth United. Produced by Peter Snell. Directed by Stuart Burge. Screenplay adapted from Shakespeare's play by Robert Furnival. Cast: Charlton Heston, Jason Robards, John Gielgud, Richard Johnson, Robert Vaughn, Richard Chamberlain, Diana Rigg, Jill Bennett, Christopher Lee.

*The Omega Man* Warner Bros. Produced by Walter Seltzer. Directed by Boris Sagal. Screenplay by John William Corrington and Joyce H. Corrington, from the novel *I Am Legend* by Richard Matheson. Cast: Charlton Heston, Anthony Zerbe, Rosalind Cash, Paul Koslo.

**1972**

*Antony and Cleopatra* Transac (Zurich)/Izaro (Madrid)/Folio Films (London). Produced by Peter Snell. Directed and adapted for the screen by Charlton Heston, from the play by William Shakespeare. Cast: Charlton Heston, Hildegard Neil, Eric Porter, John Castle, Fernando Rey, Juan Luis Galiardo, Freddie Jones, Julian Glover, Douglas Wilmer.

*Skyjacked*  MGM. Produced by Walter Seltzer. Directed by John Guillermin. Screenplay by Stanley R. Greenberg, from the novel *Hijacked* by David Harper. Cast: Charlton Heston, Yvette Mimieux, James Brolin, Claude Akins, Jeanne Crain, Walter Pidgeon.

*Call Of The Wild*  Massfilms (London)/CCC Filmkunst (Berlin)/ Izaro (Madrid)/Oceania (Rome)/UPF (Paris). Produced by Harry Alan Towers. Directed by Ken Annakin. Screenplay by Peter Welbeck (alias of Harry Alan Towers), Wyn Wells and Peter Yeldman, from the book by Jack London. Cast: Charlton Heston, Michele Mercier, Raimund Harmstorf, George Eastman.

**1973**

*Soylent Green*  MGM. Produced by Walter Seltzer and Russell Thacher. Directed by Richard Fleischer. Screenplay by Stanley R. Greenberg, from the novel *Make Room! Make Room!* by Harry Harrison. Cast: Charlton Heston, Leigh Taylor-Young, Edward G. Robinson, Chuck Connors, Joseph Cotten.

*The Three Musketeers* (and *The Four Musketeers* 1974) 20th Century-Fox. Produced by Alexander Salkind. Directed by Richard Lester. Screenplay by George MacDonald Fraser, from the novel by Alexander Dumas. Cast: Michael York, Oliver Reed, Raquel Welch, Richard Chamberlain, Frank Finlay, Charlton Heston, Faye Dunaway, Christopher Lee, Geraldine Chaplin, Jean-Pierre Cassel, Spike Milligan.

**1974**

*Earthquake*  Universal. Produced and directed by Mark Robson. Screenplay by George Fox. Cast: Charlton Heston, Ava Gardner, George Kennedy, Lorne Green, Geneviève Bujold, Richard Roundtree, Marjoe Gortner, Victoria Principal.

**1975**

*Airport 1975*  Universal. Produced by Bill Frye. Directed by Jack Smight. Screenplay by Don Ingalls. Cast: Charlton Heston, Karen Black, George Kennedy, Susan Clark, Gloria Swanson, Linda

Blair, Efrem Zimbalist Junior, Roy Thinnes, Myrna Loy, Dana Andrews, Nancy Olson, Martha Scott, Sid Caesar, Linda Harrison, Helen Reddy.

## 1976

*The Last Hard Men*   20th Century-Fox. Produced by Russell Thacher and Walter Seltzer. Directed by Andrew V. McLaglen. Screenplay by Guerdon Trueblood. Cast: Charlton Heston, James Coburn, Barbara Hershey, Christopher Mitchum, Jorge Rivero, Michael Parks.

*Midway* (GB title *Battle of Midway*)   Universal. Produced by Walter Mirisch. Directed by Jack Smight. Screenplay by Donald S. Sanford. Cast: Charlton Heston, Henry Fonda, Toshiro Mifune, Edward Albert, Robert Mitchum, James Shigeta, Christina Kokubo, James Coburn, Glenn Ford, Hal Holbrook, Cliff Robertson, Ed Nelson, Robert Wagner, Robert Webber, Kevin Dobson.

*Two-Minute Warning*   Universal. Produced by Edward S. Feldman. Directed by Larry Peerce. Screenplay by Edward Hume from the novel by George La Fountaine. Cast: Charlton Heston, John Cassavetes, Beau Bridges, Martin Balsam, Jack Klugman, Gena Rowlands, David Janssen, David Groh, Joe Kapp, Walter Pidgeon, Marilyn Hassett, Brock Peters, Mitchell Ryan.

## 1977

*The Prince and the Pauper* (also known as *Crossed Swords*)   Rank. Produced by Alexander Salkind. Directed by Richard Fleischer. Screenplay by George MacDonald Fraser. Cast: Oliver Reed, Mark Lester, Charlton Heston, Ernest Borgnine, Rex Harrison, George C. Scott, David Hemmings, Raquel Welch.

## 1978

*Gray Lady Down*   Universal. Produced by Walter Mirisch. Directed by David Greene. Screenplay by James Whittaker and Howard Sackler, from the novel *Event 1000* by David Levallee. Cast: Charlton Heston, Stacy Keach, David Carradine, Ned Beatty, Stephen Hattie, Ronny Cox, Dorian Harewood, Rosemary Forsyth.

**1979**

*The Mountain Men* Columbia. Produced by Martin Shafer and Andrew Scheinman. Directed by Richard Lang. Screenplay by Fraser Heston. Cast: Charlton Heston, Brian Keith, Victoria Racimo, Stephen Macht, John Glover, Seymour Cassel.

**1980**

*The Awakening* EMI-Orion. Produced by Robert Solo. Directed by Mike Newell. Screenplay by Allan Scott, Chris Bryant and Clive Exton. Cast: Charlton Heston, Susannah York, Jill Townsend, Stephanie Zimbalist, Patrick Dury, Bruce Myers.

**1982**

*Mother Lode* Manson International. Produced and written by Fraser Heston. Directed by Charlton Heston. Cast: Charlton Heston, Nick Mancuso, Kim Basinger, John Marley, Dale Wilson.

# Stage Plays

**1947** *State of the Union, The Glass Menagerie, Kiss and Tell*, performed at the Thomas Wolfe Memorial Theater, Ashville, North Carolina, directed by Charlton Heston.

**1948** *Antony and Cleopatra* at the Martha Beck Theater on Broadway, directed by Guthrie McClintic, with Katharine Cornell and Geoffrey Terle.
*Leaf and Bough* in Boston and on Broadway.

**1949** *Design for a Stained Glass Window* with Martha Scott in New York.

**1952** *Macbeth* in Bermuda directed by Burgess Meredith.

**1954** *Mr Roberts* by Joshua Logan, at Palm Beach, directed by Michael Howard.

**1956** *Mr Roberts* at the Casino Theater, Newport.
*Mr Roberts* at the City Center, New York, directed by John Forsythe, with Bill Harrington, Orson Bean and Fred Clark.
*Detective Story* by Sidney Kingsley on stock tour with Lydia Clarke (Heston).

**1959** *Macbeth* at Ann Arbor, Michigan with Jaqueline Brooks, directed by John O'Shaughnessy.
*State of the Union* at Santa Barbara, with Lydia Clarke.

**1960** *The Tumbler* by Benn Levy, directed by Laurence Olivier, with Martha Scott, in Boston and on Broadway.
**1965** *A Man For All Seasons* by Robert Bolt in Chicago with Lydia Clarke.
**1966** *A Man For All Seasons* at the Valley Music Theater, Los Angeles and in Miami, directed by Christopher Carey.
**1972** *The Crucible* by Arthur Miller, presented at the Ahmanson Theater, Los Angeles by Robert Fryer.
**1975** *Macbeth* at the Ahmanson, directed by Peter Wood, with Vanessa Redgrave.
**1977** *Long Day's Journey into Night* by Eugene O'Neill, presented by Robert Fryer at the Ahmanson, with Deborah Kerr and Bruce Dern, directed by Peter Wood.
**1979** *A Man For All Seasons*, presented by Robert Fryer at the Ahmanson.
**1981** *Crucifer of Blood* presented by Robert Fryer at the Ahmanson.
**1985** *The Caine Mutiny Court-Martial* by Herman Wouk, on tour in the UK and at the Queen's Theatre, London, with Ben Cross, directed by Charlton Heston.

# Television Productions

**1948** *Julius Caesar* for CBS's Studio One
*Jane Eyre* for CBS
*Of Human Bondage* for CBS
**1949** *Wuthering Heights* for CBS
*Macbeth* for CBS
*The Taming of the Shrew* for CBS
**1956** *Forbidden Area* for Playhouse 90
**1957** *The Anderson Court-Martial* for CBS
*Beauty and the Beast* for CBS
**1958** *Point Of No Return* for Playhouse 90
**1963** *The Patriots* for Hallmark
**1967** *Elizabeth and Essex* for Hallmark
**1983** *Once upon a Murder* a three-part filmed mini-series.

# Index

Page numbers in *italics* refer to entries in the filmography, where full credits are given. Heston's films will be found as main entries under the names of the films. Alphabetical arrangement is letter-by-letter.